Breaking the Deadly Embrace of Child Abuse

Breaking the Deadly Embrace of Child Abuse

E. Clay Jorgensen

Foreword by William Van Ornum

Crossroad • New York

1992

The Crossroad Publishing Company
370 Lexington Avenue
New York, NY 10017

Printed in the United States of America

Library of Congress Cataloging-in-Publication Data

Jorgensen, E. Clay.
    [Child abuse]
    Breaking the deadly embrace of child abuse / E. Clay Jorgensen ;
foreword by William Van Ornum.
        p.   cm.
    Originally published: Child abuse. New York : Continuum, 1990.
    Includes bibliographical references (p.   ).
    ISBN 0-8245-1214-6 (pbk.)
    1. Abused children—Counseling of.   2. Abusive parents—
Counseling of.   I. Title.
    HV713.J67   1992
    362.7'686—dc20   92-15508
                                                                    CIP

Contents

Foreword

Breaking the Deadly Embrace of Child Abuse

Child abuse is neither a recent discovery nor a contemporary problem. Mark Twain wrote eloquently about child abuse in *Huckleberry Finn:* Huck, beaten and left to fend for himself by his alcoholic father, escapes to a life on the river with Tom Sawyer and Jim. They have many adventures, and in the end Huck opts to head "out West" rather than live by the rules of the small-town adults.

While some abused children may recognize the possibility of a better life, very few can lead themselves toward this goal on their own. They depend on adults to bring to them the security and comfort needed to grow. While many therapists will work with abused children, greater is the number of concerned adults in each child's life. "This book," writes Dr. Jorgensen, "is written in hopes of making the work with abuse easier for 'front-line' people; those who do not have the luxury of theorizing about abuse or dealing with it through numbers or statistics or dollars. It is for child care workers, teachers, nurses, counselors, ministers, neighbors, grandparents, and friends, as well as all others who have had to experience firsthand the destruction and pain caused by child abuse."

The inner world of abused children differs from the facade they present to the world; Clay Jorgensen helps us to enter their world. This book is a fiercely empathic and compassionate portrayal of the lives of abused children and their families, with valuable practical *strategies* for all helpers. It emphasizes the importance of working to make the entire family stronger in situations where abuse occurs. Many helpers are initially angry toward the parents, but this attitude is counterproductive in the long run, because the parents must ultimately be helped if the abuse is to stop. Dr. Jorgensen provides approaches to understand and assist both the children and the parents.

Psychologists, social workers, and other therapists are often called on for support by the front-line workers in child care, teaching, or the ministry. This book will help these clinicians to "help the helpers" in a field where there is burnout, dissatisfaction, and sometimes cynicism. By making clear that our goals in these situations must always be modest, Jorgensen enables helpers to develop realistic expectations of what their interventions can produce.

Workers in child-protective services, residential treatment, and other agencies specializing in working with abused children will find this volume an especially practical resource for their work. Therapists will welcome Jorgensen's discussions on "Therapy with Children" and "Therapy with Parents." Front-line helpers will benefit from these chapters because of the information they will obtain about what happens in therapy. "Special Problems" offers the perspective of an experienced mental health clinician in responding to the psychoses, personality disorders, or alcohol and substance abuse problems that may occur in abusive families, and the care and treatment of which is essential for everyone's benefit. Issues of sexual abuse—because of their complexity—will be dealt with in a future volume.

Clay Jorgensen's dedication toward and concern for families infuses every page of this book. His twenty years' experience of working in the field makes him an eminently helpful guide and mentor for the rest of us. He recognizes that, in facing child abuse, we are saddened—but that to withdraw or despair does not help. His effective insights will provide hope to the helpers, children, and families whose lives are affected by abuse.

William Van Ornum, Ph.D.
Marist College
Poughkeepsie, New York

General Editor

Acknowledgments

I wish to acknowledge my indebtedness to many people who facilitated the writing of this book. I am indebted to and appreciate the opportunity afforded by the Spokane Community Mental Health Center which for twenty years has allowed me an arena in which to learn about child abuse, and to the many people, both children and parents, who patiently shared their worlds with me and taught me what I know. I wish to thank those who contributed directly to the writing through encouragment and suggestions, especially Dr. William Van Ornum, Chris Crutcher, and Dr. Mary Dietzen. I wish to thank Janice McGalliard who typed the drafts. Finally, I wish to express my appreciation and thanks to my wife, Doris, and children, Elmer, Layne, Rhonda, Julia, and Sheila, whose support and love kept me from going crazy during periods of stress and despair, both in my writing and in my work with abusing families.

Author's Note

The identities of the people written about in this book have been carefully disguised in accordance with professional standards of confidentiality and in keeping with their rights to privileged communication with the author.

Introduction: Night-Light

When I was a child, I had a night-light. It was one of those that plugged into a socket behind my bed and was shaped like Mickey Mouse. I had it for years and would never have considered going to bed without it being on. I had terrible nightmares about monsters getting me, and would wake up screaming. I was always afraid of the dark and imagined all kinds of horrible things lurking in the darkness waiting to get me. The light made me feel safer. I don't even remember how old I was when I got Mickey, but I must have been pretty young. I remember it had a part chipped out in the head, shaped like a long, thin triangle. I don't remember how that happened; it seemed like it was always there. It used to bother me that it was broken, and once I put Scotch tape over the hole—but the heat of the light burned it off after a few nights.

I didn't like it that it was broken until the day I got my arm broke. Actually, my father broke my arm although he denied it. I was always afraid of my father, who back then seemed gigantic. He was always raging about one thing or another that went wrong. Once he tried to fix my bicycle. He couldn't get a part or something on and threw the bike and stomped it until it was a mass of twisted junk. He tore his pants and shirt in the process until they hung on him in shreds. He had a triumphant gleam in his eyes and it seemed like it had been a satisfying experience for him.

He would hit me or punch me for things I did wrong. I did things wrong most of the time; bring him the wrong wrench, not make my bed quite good enough, interrupt when adults were talking and at times for reasons I didn't know and had better sense than to ask. About the worst he had hurt me before he broke my arm was when we were at the dinner table and I giggled because my brother said "Pass the graby" (he had trouble with v's). I was sitting around the corner from my dad at the table and he back-handed me, knocking me and the chair over. I hit my head and was dizzy for a few days. My mother yelled at him (which was unusual since mostly she whined or got a headache and went to her room when he was in a rage). He was pretty nice for a few days after that.

The day he broke my arm he had told me to go to the basement and pack a bunch of empty mason jars in boxes and put them in the kitchen so he could load them in the pickup and take them to my grandmother. My grandmother canned stuff for us. I decided to please my father and went and packed all of the bottles, but instead of leaving them in the kitchen, I put them in the truck for him. I then went (without being told) and wiped off the shelves where the bottles had been and dust had collected, and then I cleaned the basement. All this took about an hour. I had just come up the stairs from the basement and opened the door between the basement and the kitchen when I saw my father looming there in the doorway, his face dark with rage with that triumphant gleam in his eyes. I was scared and started to ask what was wrong when his fist caught me in the chest and I went down the stairs. My arm hit under me on the corner of the stair, and I heard it snap. I remember being dazed and it seemed like I was looking through a tunnel at my arm thinking how curious it was, it looked like I had two elbows. I think my father not seeing the boxes of bottles in the kitchen assumed I hadn't done the job. He told my mother I slipped, which she was relieved to believe. I didn't dare say anything different. The doctor who set my arm wasn't curious about how it happened or had accepted my parents' explanation, anyway I never said anything about it.

I remember that night after my arm got broke, laying in the bed being struck with how pleased I was that my Mickey Mouse light had a crack in it. It made us the same. We were both broken and we were friends.

—extracted from a personal history written by a young adult on entering counseling for his own abusive behavior

As a psychologist in a mental health center years ago, I encountered my first case of severe child abuse. This was during my first year of actual applied work and I was as green as grass. A mother with an eight-year-old boy was referred to me by her son's school for a variety of behavior problems including enuresis, encopresis, school failure, food hoarding, stealing, and other rebellious, disobedient behaviors. Particularly aggravating to the mother was the boy's habit of tossing the lunch she packed for him each day into a culvert and then begging food from other children and teachers.

When I met with the child, I noticed he had bumps on his head and facial bruises. His mother readily admitted causing the injuries in her attempts to "correct" the boy. This was back in 1966, before the acute public (and for that matter, professional) awareness of child abuse and before enactment of the state of Washington's child abuse reporting laws. I knew something was terribly wrong. Aside from the bruises and bumps, the child's eyes haunted me. His look of desperate confusion and self-hatred was appalling, and I felt I had to do something. His mother obviously considered the problem to be strictly a matter of an unruly son and she had no insight into the fact that her abusive approach was perpetuating the problem and making it worse. My suggestion that she try positive reinforcement for "good" behavior was rejected out of hand with the comment that she did not believe in "bribing" children. She thwarted my efforts to get her to talk about herself, her own fears and frustrations, by stating simply that her only problem was "the kid."

I finally prevailed on her to try using a time-out procedure as an alternative to physical punishment and hitting. Any hope for this approach was deflated when, at the next appointment, she triumphantly announced that she had confined the boy to his room for a solid week—her interpretation of time-out—without any improvement in her son's behavior. She quit coming after the third session: It was obvious to her that I did not "understand the problem." I don't know what happened to the boy, but I have been tortured by my memory of him and how helpless I was to do anything about what he was going through.

Today, with the child abuse statutes that exist in every state and the variety of laws designed to protect children, such scenarios are unlikely. Children are no longer considered chattel to be treated in whatever manner a parent wishes. The laws and statutes, however, have in no way solved the problem. They have simply driven it to the surface and to that extent made it more accessible. There has been criticism from some parents' rights groups that these laws have resulted in too much interference with family life and parental authority, and it is true that families have undoubtedly been abused through a zealous application of the laws. Nevertheless, the effect has generally been helpful to children and, whether acknowledged or not, helpful to families in the long run. If misuses and excesses are permitted or encouraged by the current laws, they in no way justify a return to the time when children were considered property and frequently maltreated and when animals had more protection under our laws than they did.

The problem remains, however, to find solutions to the basic dilemma of abuse. Abuse affects all of us. It makes the jobs of teachers more difficult. It creates an unknown quantity of health problems and associated health costs. (Parenthetically, the health costs of treating injuries caused by abuse is minuscule compared to the costs, medical *and* psychological, created by the psychological distress and damage resulting to children and parents because of abuse.) It plays the major role in filling our penal facilities, our counseling facilities, and our welfare rolls. It steals childhood from children and defiles the parenting experience. It savages families, individual lives, and dreams. There is no more virulent, destructive epidemic.

My own introduction to child abuse came gradually and stealthfully. In a sense, I grew up with it professionally. In my work, at least in the early years, people came to me with problems they identified as child misbehaviors, including such things as enuresis, encopresis, night terrors and other sleeping disturbances, school failure, social isolation, and hyperactivity. Frequently I discovered an underlying pattern of abusive behavior that was experienced by the parents as either their normal frustration response to their child's behavior problems, or simply "the way you handle kids." As I struggled to work with these families, I gradually discarded abhorrence and blaming of parents as nonhelpful, appealing to reason as irrelevant, and empathic understanding as nice but ineffectual. The circular, mutually exacerbating nature of child and parent behavior, the traps forged by lifelong experiences and attitudes, which became apparent, led me to discard blaming and faulting in favor of active intervention focused on both child and parent behavior, thinking and feeling, and on the complex interaction between them.

This book is written in the hope of making the work with abuse easier for front-line people, those who do not have the luxury of theorizing about abuse or dealing with it through numbers or statistics or dollars. It is for child care workers, teachers, nurses, counselors, ministers, neighbors, grandparents, friends, and parents—as well as for all others who have had to experience, firsthand, the destruction and pain caused by child abuse. It offers no final answers or solutions. The goals are modest: help with understanding the problem, help with directions for working with children and parents, and help with making that task more tolerable.

1

The Abuse Embrace

Hunters and hikers in the West have at times encountered the remains of two bull elk that have perished in their rut battles, horns still locked. Finders of these enmeshed racks of horns can often separate the horns by pushing them together and twisting them free; something the animals in their rage and fear could not or would not do. Abusing families are similarly joined in a deadly embrace, child and parents locked in their dilemma of anger, fear, and confusion and without means to break the cycle.

It is popular to try to solve problems and interpret tragedies through identifying and labeling a *victim* and a *perpetrator*. Generally, this approach is useless in dealing with problems of poverty, international politics, and marriage, and it is especially useless in dealing with child abuse. Abusing parents can legitimately be described as victims in a variety of arenas in their life. Certainly they are victimized by the cycle of abuse in their own families. They are, at the same time, perpetrators *and* victims. They hurt their children at times in devastating, almost incomprehensible ways. The damage they do to their own self-esteem, peace of mind, and success in life is less obvious—but just as grievous.

As devastating as physical injuries are to children, usually the most damaging, permanent, and difficult injuries are psychological in nature. The confusion, fear, distorted attitudes, and destructive coping patterns developed by

21

their children in response to abuse constitutes a legacy that can serve to block achievement and distort interpersonal relationships for the remainder of their lives. This psychological damage is also the seedbed from which a new generation of abuse grows and flourishes and is a curse handed down by abusing parents to their children.

For the most part, abusing parents see themselves responding in the only way they can to the circumstances they confront. They react to their children's behavior with the faulty tools (attitudes, discipline-approaches, and expectations) that they have been given. They become increasingly frustrated, angry, and desperate, and their response to their children's behavior ultimately becomes increasingly deviant and destructive. In other words, abuse leads to problem behaviors in children, which lead to escalating abuse by parents. Both children and parents feel trapped in this cycle, and both feel cheated, discounted, and misunderstood. They are, at the same time, angry and helpless.

Alex, an intense young father who had beaten his two boys, ages 3 and 5 with a belt, said in a counseling interview: "I remember my father beating me with a belt and I know it was a bad thing to do, but at the time, I just lost control. I don't know if I was mad at the kids or mad at my dad—it was all confusing. I didn't know what to do. . . . I feel like a criminal."

In working with child abuse, it is important to focus on both parents and child. It is difficult, if not impossible, to fully salvage one without the other. One tool available to "rescue" a child from abuse is removing him or her from the parents and terminating parental rights. While in most cases where such termination is done, it will prevent future abuse by the parents, enough damage has already occurred to the child psychologically that he or she will continue to have problems the rest of his or her life. While in some cases the child (particularly a young child) can be successfully grafted into a loving, nurturing family, the record of successful adoptions or foster care of children is spotty at best and the child is left to cope with the disturbing questions at a later time as to why he or she was "abused" or "abandoned" by the natural parents.

Seventeen-year-old Angela, who was placed with a foster family at age two and subsequently adopted by that family after her abusing parents relinquished custody, said: "My mom and dad have been good to me and they are really my parents—in my feelings, I mean. But I wonder why my real parents didn't want me. . . . I feel that there msut have been something wrong with me.

There are, of course, times when permanent removal of a child from the parent(s) is the only safe option.

2

Emotional Abuse

In some respects violent, assaultive behavior on the part of parents is the symptom of the abuse disease. Emotional abuse is the virus. It is both an inevitable consequence of all other kinds of abuse and neglect and is the source of the parents' abusive behavior.

There is an imbalance in our society in our reactions, respectively, to sexual, physical, and emotional abuse. As reflected in everything from media accounts and coverage to court decisions, we are enraged and sickened by sexual abuse, in whatever degree of severity. We have these same reactions to instances in which physical abuse has resulted in death or crippling injury. Apart from these two scenarios, however, our reactions too often fall within a range of moderate concern to indifference.

Emotional abuse, in particular, gets occasional lip service but by and large is not the subject of indignation, laws, rhetoric, or outrage in our society. This is the case, despite the fact that the major vehicle of damage to children—regardless of the specific abuse—is, in fact, the emotional devastation that accompanies the abuse. A good portion of this emotional damage, especially in the case of sexual abuse, derives from the reactions of adults to the abuse and from the investigation and legal processes that occur following such instances of abuse. Obviously, physical maltreatment that results in death and permanent injury, and sexual assault that includes penetration of the child, in and of themselves are terribly damaging. However, the bulk of physical harm consists of inflicting pain and temporary injuries rather than death and permanent malfunction. The majority of cases of sexual abuse involve touching and fondling rather than penetration. Nevertheless, in all cases there are permanent or long-term emotional injuries to the child, including self-depreciation, loss of security, fear and a feeling of helplessness, self-blame, and self-hatred. Such long-term or permanent emotional injuries are inflicted on many children daily—without real physical or sexual abuse—and probably these instances far outnumber the cases of the other two kinds of abuse. They are, moreover, less easily observed and less reliably or objectively defined or measured. This lack of objective measurement, however, does not lessen the extent of their harm to children.

Professionals who work with sexually or physically abused children recognize that sexual and physical abuse result in legacies of emotional damage. Still, the link between the child's emotional problems and the parents' behavior—an essential element in legal intervention—is much more clear and tangible where specific acts of hitting, burning, or sexually assaulting the child can be identified. If the child shows signs of emotional disturbance *and* if there is more or less objective proof that the parent has hit or sexually touched the child, there is less difficulty determining that that behavior caused the emotional harm, which, in turn, allows for intervention. Where there is no evidence of hitting or sexual touching, etc., the child's emotional problems or damage are less likely to be credibly linked to the parents' behavior, however emotionally abusive that behavior has been.

This disparity in reaction and response (legal and otherwise) to emotional abuse versus sexual or physical abuse exists because the legal system—the primary intervention machinery and authority—is based on objective evidence. Truth is defined by what we can observe clearly and can measure. As a society, we deal best with those things that lend themselves to "objectivity" or are easiest to observe, and those things less easily observed or measured get less attention and study and lend themselves less readily to intervention. Our preference for the objective over the subjective despite the frequent greater importance of the subjective is illustrated in the following story:

> There were two friends strolling along a street at night talking. One was a clear-eyed, hard-headed scientist who dealt in facts, evidence, and objective reality. The other was a rather fuzzy-thinking philosopher who dealt with ideas, theories, and subjective reality. This was long ago, when streets had gas lights on the corners that cast a pool of light only a few yards in circumference at each corner. In between these pools of light, the streets were very dark. While walking along the street at a point midway between the corners, one of the friends dropped a valuable gold watch. The scientist went immediately to the corner to look for the watch because that is where the light enabled him to see. The philosopher dropped on his hands and knees and began groping around in the dark because that is where the watch was.

We need to expend more effort groping around in the dark of emotional abuse because that is where the long-term or permanent damage to children occurs.

Another major reason for the disparity between our reaction to sexual abuse and other kinds of abuse, including emotional, derives from our puritanical roots. These roots suggest to us that sexuality is the most abhorrent and serious threat to human welfare and salvation. At the same time, punishment—including physical violence, ostracism, induction of guilt, and social shunning—are historically seen as appropriate, and even necessary, remedial activities for sexual misconduct. People guilty of sexual sins have in the past been severely punished and even, in distant times, put to death.

This attitude toward sex is alive and well and exists as an undercurrent in our society. The attitude towards sex and violence is apparent in the hue and cry often heard for the physical punishment, and even death, of sexual offenders. No one, on the other hand, recommends sexual molesting or sexual violation as punishment for people who beat or kill their children. An exposed breast in a movie will result in an "R" rating, while a couple of good fights with the good buys beating up on the bad guys will not result in an "PG-13" or "R" rating (unless there is an excessive amount of gore).

Emotional abuse consists of actions on the part of parents or caretakers that are depreciating of the child, make the child fearful, stop the developmental processes, or result in emotional disturbance.

3

Working with the Child

Sometimes I get so scared about life that I wish I could crawl in a nice warm hole and pull the dirt in after me. People frighten me more than anything. They can be so evil and scheming, that I wish I could escape. Sometimes when I am alone I dream of how wonderful things could be if love were behind each person's motives and words instead of hate, greed, and jealousy. Although life is complicated, my heart gets so keyed up at times that I have to run because I'm alive and I'm able. But never fast enough. My heart seems miles away from my body. I feel that if I wanted to I could lift up and soar through the sky like a bird. It is such things as the wind, night, snow, and rain that give me great satisfaction. Just as physically I have to express myself, I must use mental expression. I love to sit in my room and write down every thought, every sensation I get. Pouring out my heart in love can also relieve the pressures, and daydreaming stops the pain. I even find myself daydreaming during class but still listening to every word. I think every one needs self-expression and an escape route in order to succeed in life.

—*"I Have to Run," by an anonymous 13-year-old*

Working with abused children can be rewarding but it can also be frustrating and frightening. Considering what these children have been through, it is a terrible responsibility, not to be taken lightly. Working with abused children is for either good or evil; it is seldom neutral.

Working with such children requires skill and understanding, but above all it requires empathy and the patience of Job. Reactions and behaviors of abused children are incomprehensible unless we understand the child's world through the child's eyes. That world is, at times, very different from what we expect, even knowing something about his or her traumas and other life experiences.

Understanding, or empathy, constitutes just the first step, however. It is necessary to have an overall vision of what the child is about, a sense of direction for working with the child and tools to help the child. Taking a page from medical ethics, the first rule is "Do no harm." Beyond that, those who work with children have an obligation to protect them and enable them to experience not just freedom from fear and pain, but also to experience success, joy, and growth.

Advertising programs for abused children often use pictures of young children between the ages of two and five with a tear in the corner of one of their enormous, appealing eyes. While the intent is to generate deserved sympathy for the plight of children in abusive situations, it gives the unintended and incorrect message that such children are attractive, that they differ from other children only in respect to their pain. On the contrary, while these children are in pain they are usually *not* attractive; and their behavior is *not* like that of other children. They are—typically—obnoxious children, who react to attempts to help them with anxiety, fear, and misbehavior. They often "bite" the extended, helping hand.

One of the first myths about abused children confronted by people who work with them is that the child will respond immediately and openly to kindness, love, and good intentions. Where their abuse has been severe and prolonged, such children cannot afford the trust that this responsiveness demands. They have pent-up rage that cripples their ability to respond to love. They are children without self-respect, empathy for others, or the anticipation of reward that would enable them to appreciate others' good intentions. They have come to see people as being dangerous, undependable, and unrewarding—and they react accordingly.

Jerri and Ben, a handsome, religious, middle-class couple, had raised two model children. Their son, a senior in high school, was a popular athlete and their daughter, a sophomore in college, was a pretty and popular straight-A pre-med student. The couple had achieved economic stability and social and family success and decided to extend the benefits of their nurturing, loving home to foster children, possibly with the view toward adoption. Through an agency that handles preadoptive placements for difficult children, they took into their home three-year-old twin girls, Anne and Amy. These children were Amerasian and had been severely abused and neglected; they had eventually been abandoned by their Vietnamese mother after she was abandoned by her serviceman husband.

After three months of placement, the couple requested that the children be taken from their home because of behavior problems. In a debriefing interview, Jerri stated, "They are impossible. They constantly wet the bed and mess their pants, and nothing I did seemed to work. They destroyed things and threw tantrums. We gave them all of the love any child could want. I made matching dresses for them and Anne cut them up with scissors. We never had any trouble with our own children. I just can't understand it. I knew that they had been abused and I expected some problems, but when I found myself constantly screaming at them and wanting to hit them, I knew I couldn't go on [with the placement]."

Many a well-meaning foster-parent couple have had

their confidence in their patience and parenting ability shaken by abused children. Failed foster-care or adoptive placements for these children is, of course, extremely damaging to them.

A second myth about abused children is that they will appreciate efforts to help them. Many of these kids have been in, what for them, is a life-and-death struggle. They have experienced others as capricious and unpredictable, and the absence of hitting or other abuse is for them merely an undependable period of respite until they are hurt again. Children cannot appreciate until they can feel appreciated, they cannot trust until the world is predictable, and they cannot love until they feel both lovable and loved.

A professional speaking about twenty years of experiences in working with abused children and their families has said:

> At times, it has been very discouraging. The parents are usually defensive and angry, at least initially, and the children are sometimes so damaged that the work feels overwhelming. These kids need love, acceptance, and understanding so much and yet when it is offered, it seems to frighten and confuse them. They test over and over again your patience and caring. It helped, once I realized that my job was to aid these families so that the abuse stops and they are able to develop intellectually and emotionally in a more or less normal way. Whether or not they appreciated my efforts and my worry about them was unimportant. Just seeing some of them get out of the destructive cycle they were in and experience more feelings of success and self-worth was all the reward I needed. Sometimes even that was hard to come by. All in all, these families have taught me

a lot, not only in a professional sense, but about myself. It has been humbling, but in the final analysis
it has been worth the effort and pain.

Marie, a 26-year-old woman who had been an abused
child, has talked about her experiences in foster care and
therapy when she was an adolescent:

> I guess I went through . . . oh, about six foster homes
> and maybe six or eight therapists. I can't remember
> them all. . . . Some of my life then seems like a blur.
> I was so angry at my parents, the world, anyone who
> got in range. The people who wanted to help me
> so much—they were the easiest targets. I never
> trusted that they really cared about me. I always
> thought I was some kind of a "case" to them. I would
> do rotten, terrible things—partly because I just had
> to express how angry I was and partly to see if they
> could prove they really cared. Once I fed some baby
> goats Styrofoam and it killed them. These were prize
> goats that the family I lived with had. The people
> drug me right down to the Welfare office and left
> me in the waiting room for my caseworker.
> People would give up on me, and while it seemed
> like that is what I wanted—at least that's what I always
> said—I always felt secretly disappointed and hurt that
> it hadn't worked out and I had to leave. I remember
> that Molly [the last foster parent with whom Marie
> lived for the last two years of high school] telling me
> once that "No matter what you do, you're stuck with
> me . . . I'm not going to give up." I acted mad about
> it, but secretly I was pleased.

A third myth about abused children and abusing families
is that the abuse is constant and unremitting. This, of
course, is not the case. Generally, abuse occurs sporadi-
cally and is triggered by various stresses and high-tension

situations. Harold, who was abused to the point where he was hospitalized twice as a child, remembers:

> While we never talked about it, we knew that Dad was going to be looking for an excuse to hit us whenever he and Mom had a fight or whenever he had to pay bills. All us kids had an understanding that during these times we were quiet and stayed out of his way as much as possible. My brother and I, who is a year younger than me, even learned how to fight quietly. We were kind of competitive and at times would get into disagreements, but if we made any noise, then all hell would break loose, and so we could have pretty serious fights without making any noise at all.

Abusing families behave, especially in public, the way other families behave. They go out to dinner, work in the yard, go to church, and have pleasant and rewarding times. What is different about them is the sporadic episodes of violence or neglect, the rather consistent denigration and disparagement (usually of the children by one or both parents), and the psychological scars and dysfunction that the abuse creates for all the family. As stated by Josh, a rather insightful but withdrawn seventeen-year-old, when talking about his family (including an angry, abusive father): "He treated other people great. They loved him and thought he was such a great guy. They never saw him when he was in a rage. He could be screaming at me and knocking me around, and someone would come to the door—a neighbor or something—and just like that he would be all smiles and just gush friendliness and charm."

Working with abused children in whatever arena or role requires a combination of understanding, caring, and perseverance. It means working with people who are angry, who are unappreciative, and who are at times unpleasant. Success comes through serial small victories in private and without accolade or honor, rather than in large, acknowledged victories. It means being satisfied with scant recognition and living with consistent frustration and worry.

Children react in unique ways to abuse, but there is a common core of acceptance, confusion, indifference, rage, incompetence, and self-hatred experienced by abused children.

Acceptance. To understand the child's experience with abuse, we have to understand that the child measures his experiences inside a vacuum. The child usually does not have a background of experience with a consistent, safe, nurtured life against which to judge the abuse to be unusual, aberrant, or undeserved. The child experiences the abuse as painful, frightening, and confusing, but cannot see (as we do) that it is something outside of himself, something that is aberrant. Five-year-old Sarah, a somber, dark-haired child expresses this clearly: "My mom only hits me when I'm bad. . . . But sometimes she likes me—if I be good."

The child blames himself, feeling he is deserving of maltreatment or that this is the order of things to be endured or handled by whatever means he can find. He often feels undeserving of better treatment, and during periods of reprieve from abuse he may begin to feel uneasy and even guilty.

Confusion. The child is confused not so much because he is abused but because the abuse is unpredictable. He may be hurt, praised, or ignored at different times for the same behavior and apparently under the same circumstances. He has no awareness of the ebb and flow of the parents' frustrations and confusion that results in inconsistent treatment, and is he left struggling to find some way to understand the conditions that lead to the violent, frightening behavior on the part of his parents.

Ken, whose lanky, good-humored style hides intense self-doubt and anger—the result of his childhood battering by both parents—says:

> I used to lie awake at nights waiting for my parents to come home (usually from a night of drinking), wondering if I had done anything that they would hit me for. Sometimes they would be mad about some little thing, and sometimes big things I did wrong didn't seem to bother them. Once, when I forgot to shut off the sprinkler, they took turns beating me with a belt. Another time, I played with matches in the garage and started a fire. I got the fire out. They didn't even say anything about that.

Indifference. One of the puzzling things about children who have experienced consistent or frequent abuse is that they seem to become immune to being hurt. Abusing parents complain that the child no longer shows reaction to their "punishment," and this often leads to an escalation of hitting or other abusive behavior. The child is not so much afraid of being hurt as he is of the unpredictability of *when* he will be hurt. In a paradoxical way, children sometimes behave in ways they know will elicit abuse, simply to do away with the anxiety of not knowing when it will occur. Kids seem to learn to just switch off their feelings since they have no way of preventing the abuse. This pattern of being unfeeling or indifferent has long been noted by people working with abused children. It is a pattern that causes problems for them as adults.

Janna, a chain-smoking, nervous young woman, has spoken about her experiences with an abusive father:

When I was little, I was very scared of my dad. He had a violent temper and I could never tell what would set him off. I would do everything to please him that I could. After a while, especially when I got to be about thirteen or fourteen, I stopped trying—because it didn't do any good anyway. It started being like a game. I would do things to aggravate him and then see how far I could go (with the beatings) before I would cry or say I was sorry. I got so I could go a long way, and afterward, even though I was hurting, I had the sense of satisfaction that I held out so long.

The last time he beat me was when I was sixteen and had come home about three hours after he said I had to be home. He beat me with a belt until I was black and blue from by knees to my waist. I never did cry or apologize and after a while he just quit. I remember afterwards he looked so old and kind of defeated that I almost felt sorry for him. I ran away after that and never went back.

It has been noted by professionals that abusive parents often react most violently not to children's behavior as much as to the child's lack of remorse or "being sorry" for the misbehavior. Parents often interpret this "indifference" as stubbornness or a lack of respect for the parent rather than the self-protective emotional insulation that children develop in response to abuse. The parent does not understand that this indifference results from the abuse and that hitting the child simply leads to a *higher* threshold of indifference. Hitting children teaches them fear, not respect; it makes them resentful and angry, not remorseful.

A startled psychologist listened to twelve-year-old Emily talk about a beating administered by her stepmother, who used a belt on her buttocks and legs: "My mom said I should tell her why I was so angry and that I should express my feelings. I couldn't think of anything, so she hit me with the belt to teach me how to handle my anger better."

Martha, a nineteen-year-old single mother with three preschool-age children, had difficult problems with her four-and-a-half-year-old son, James, whom she had severely beaten with a wire hanger. "I don't understand James. He knows he'll get it if he acts up, but he does it anyway. If I spank him with my hand, he doesn't cry or say he's sorry or nothin'."

Rage. An inevitable by-product of physical pain and fear is anger. Abused children typically are enraged children. They have learned to suppress or control their rage and often express it only in indirect ways through a variety of behavior symptoms, including expressions of anger at weaker and more helpless beings than themselves, such as younger children and animals. Abused children will often express their anger in play motifs and fantasies. Sarah, age five, compulsively engages in doll play in which her fantasy scenarios always end with the mother doll being beaten, kicked, and thrown.

Adults who were abused as children often cope with their suppressed rage by selecting violent mates. They obtain some vicarious release of their own rage through their mate's violence: They are frequently the target of the spouse's violence. Often they do not protect themselves against violent partners, since they have learned to accept the victim role.

Jaime, a tall, pretty brunette, had her first child at age fifteen and a second at age seventeen. Both children were removed from her by Child Protective Services on the allegations of neglect and abuse. In the course of a court-ordered evaluation, she revealed her own history of abuse and battering, mostly by her father. She also revealed that she had been married twice and had several other "live-in" relationships. Both husbands and two boyfriends had been violent and abusive. In talking about these abusive relationships, she said, "I think I know why I get hooked up with men who are violent, like my dad. I don't go looking for them, but I'm used to being hit, so when they start being mean and hitting me I just put up with it. Sometimes I feel like I must deserve it. It also makes me . . . I don't know . . . it's like they show they care, 'cause that's the only kind of attention I got from my father. I keep hoping that they will love me enough so they *won't* hit me. I always hoped my father would love me, too."

Incompetence. In abusing families, much of the correcting done by parents revolves around the child's developing attempts at self-mastery. Since his efforts to do new things and to develop his skills often lead to criticism or harsh punishment, he develops the belief that he is not capable or is incompetent. He becomes reluctant to try new things and, as a result, is often behind or slow in developing competencies, or living skills. A consistent finding in evaluations of abused children is developmental delay and academic problems or failure. The chain of self-perception, poor performance, and negative feedback from others can lock a child into this pattern of incompetence.

John, a thirteen-year-old blond, pudgy boy with blue eyes and a bad case of acne, was one such abused child. Among his array of problems, he usually got poor or failing marks in school, was isolated from his peers, and had a very poor self-image. One element of his poor self-esteem was that he thought he was "dumb." John, in fact, acted as if he was mentally slow and fit the stereotype of what people thought "dumb" kids looked like. He tolerated being the butt of classmates' jokes and pranks, forgot assignments, and was socially inept.

While it would no longer be considered a sound practice, John, along with his seventh-grade classmates, was given a paper-and-pencil intelligence test by his homeroom teacher. The teacher had a brief conference with each student and gave them their test results in the percentile ranks. This, again, is a rather archaic practice that would not likely be done today. When it came John's turn, a puzzled teacher noting an IQ ranking at above the 95th percentile qualified it by saying, "But, of course, that is way too high for you. . . . There must have been a mistake." John was devastated; he had wanted very much to have that high score. He easily gave it up, however, since the teacher's qualifying statement about the test fit his perception of himself. It was not until years later, via a series of chance happenings leading to college work, that he was able to believe in his intelligence.

Self-hatred. Abused children hate themselves. Because of their abuse they conclude that their parents hate them, and they identify with the parents' hate. They are often self-destructive and may make suicidal gestures or attempts. They are frequently observed playing out this self-hatred in doll play: "The boy was bad"—hitting a doll—"so his mom killed 'im." A frightening recent trend has been suicides among children, and while there are usually complex causes of suicidal behavior, children who suicide or attempt it have frequently been abused and/or neglected.

Children who hate themselves very often hate others. They express this hate or anger toward others who are helpless or at least weaker than themselves. SueAnn, at age thirteen, considered herself ugly, as did her classmates, who nicknamed her "Piggy." She had a somewhat flat, upturned nose on which she and her detractors focused. SueAnn came to professional attention when she severely beat a one-year-old infant she was baby-sitting. SueAnn gave as the reason for the beating: "The baby wouldn't stop crying."

In her evaluation appointment with a psychologist, Sue-Ann was defensive, sullen, and withdrawn. She responded to questions about her school, family, and friends with a cold stare or an indifferent "I don't know." She did affirm, with a nod, that she had hurt the baby. Well into the interview, the evaluator explained to SueAnn, "For you to have hurt the baby like that, I think you must have been hurt yourself." While the psychologist meant "hurt yourself" only in a sense of emotional hurt, the statement triggered an outpouring in which SueAnn, between sobs, talked about her ugliness, rejection by classmates, and rejection and physical abuse by her stepmother. (Parenthetically, after six months of treatment at a community mental health center that focused on self-esteem, the evaluator met SueAnn by chance and initially did not recognize the pretty, happy, vivacious youngster as the previously depressed, sullen, and angry SueAnn.)

4

The Child's Coping Strategies

All children have innate fundamental drives that include self-mastery, growth, and exploration. In an abusing family these drives are as strong as they are for children in other families, but they become distorted into destructive and self-defeating patterns by the experience of abuse.

Subversion and Sabotage. The desire for self-mastery and control leads to development of power tactics by the child in an abusing family. Since abuse is unpredictable, the child will of necessity develop intense, compelling tactics to express the need for mastery or control. Among the strongest of these is a pattern of subversion and sabotage. Children in an abusing situation are effectively blocked from expressing their control through positive growth and development. They learn, however, that they can exercise considerable power and influence through their own blocking or negative approaches, and in this way can also exercise some control over their own bodies.

Children frequently refuse, for example, to engage in toilet training. They find that by retaining their own feces, by wetting the beds, by refusing to eat or keep food down they can effectively gain some measure of control that has a by-product of satisfying retaliation because it frustrates the parents' wishes. What for children in normal families is a mild struggle—given up as they experience success and a feeling of mastery in accomplishing goals

41

consistent with the parents' desires—becomes an almost life-and-death struggle to maintain control over their own bodies. Maria, a young mother talking to a counselor about her child, said, "I know that Ricky knows how to use the toilet 'cause he does it right sometimes. . . . But he'll poop anywhere. It feels like he's shitting on me."

Creative Stupidity. In like manner, abused children often engage in creative stupidity. This tactic involves refusal to learn even the simplest tasks or finding creative ways of mismanaging parental requests. The frequent result is that parents are again frustrated and blocked in their efforts to control and direct the child. Since the child will experience abuse regardless of his actions, misbehavior changes nothing in terms of the abuse he experiences. He will, however, gain some satisfaction by exercising some control over his life and retaliating against the parent in a way that is disguised.

Some workers call this tactic "crazy-making," because it makes parents crazy. Evidence of crazy-making is seen in such typical parental statements as: "It's easier to do it myself"; "I feel like he's running things and I'm a slave"; "I know he's smart, but sometimes he acts so dumb I can't believe it."

Cutting the Losses. is another strategy developed by children. Again, where abuse itself cannot be avoided but only controlled as to time and place, children learn that trying new things has a high probability of failure. They learn, then, to make halfhearted or inadequate efforts at mastery of different tasks and in this way precipitate the recrimination of negative input or abuse without having to go through the effort and pain of making a more legitimate effort. Abused kids are often seen by school personnel as slow or even retarded, or as willfully disobedient. Their school failures and behavior problems are not the result of either disobedience or mental dullness but are a strategy learned in an abusive environment.

Fading into the Woodwork. Children who are abused do everything they can to make themselves "invisible." Thus, they attempt to avoid contact with other people whenever they can. They avoid drawing attention to themselves, and as they grow older they attempt to be away from their homes as much as possible.

Joe, a stocky twelve-year-old, would spend as much time as possible sitting outside his back door in front of the dryer vent, his coat up over his head. He shyly gave a counselor an elaborate picture of a spaceship he had drawn with painstaking detail. This was the same counselor who spent most of his sessions looking at Joe's noncommunicative back in counseling sessions and to whom Joe had replied, "Don't get personal," when asked how his day had been. Through work with Joe, it was found that he was not "psychotic," as school personnel and a consulting psychiatrist had suggested, but long-term frequent physical abuse was discovered.

Defensive Interpretations. One dilemma faced by children who experience abuse is to make some kind of sense of the confusion created by their parents' behavior. They develop a variety of interpretations of their environment to aid them in making predictions about it. These conceptions and these predictions, while serving some function within the context of their disordered abusive family, tend to serve them poorly in situations outside it. One such conception is that all people are inherently unpredictable, dangerous, and potentially abusive. The child then reacts to people through withdrawal, avoidance, or the precipitation of a conflict that relieves them of the anxiety over when they will experience hurt or rejection.

Children's distorted interpretations are often aided and abetted by their parents. They see themselves as bad people deserving of abuse, and this same interpretation is offered by the parents in rationalizing their abusiveness. Abused children come to see children in general, and themselves in particular, as objects of no particular value designed for and deserving of maltreatment by older, stronger people. This conception of course gives rise to the destructive attitudes about children that often result in their becoming abusing parents, themselves, in later life.

5

Child-Helping Strategies

I think that saving a little child
And bringing him to his own,
Is a derned sight better business
Than loafing around the throne.

—John Hay

The approach used in working with a child is prescribed by the experience the child has had with abuse and the coping strategies he has developed. By the time abused children come to the attention of helping professionals or others attempting to remedy the situation, they have learned well their roles, including all the patterns of destructive, obnoxious, and difficult behavior described earlier.

Hope. The first order of business in working with an abused child is to provide some hope that things can be different. The child needs to experience foster parents or therapists or counselors or teachers in a different way than he has experienced the abusing adults in his life. The patterns of behavior he has developed that elicit negative, abusive, critical, or rejecting responses from others need to be undermined. For example, eleven-year-old Randy, recently removed from a highly abusive family, in response to the question from a counselor, "How are you doing today?" replied, "It's none of your business, this is stupid, and you're a stupid jerk." The counselor, without going into the merits of these observations, was able to reply, "You sound mad, but I think that you're mostly afraid that I might not like you".

Since the boy was anticipating that his behavior would be met with counter-anger or professionally phrased discounting and rejection, as it had in the past, he was caught by surprise and reacted with some confusion. In this exchange Randy briefly experienced not playing out the scenario of misbehavior—and rejection or abuse—that he had grown to expect, and was able to experience some new options regarding how others see him and how he could behave.

The main tool in giving abused children hope is patience. They have to test and retest their experiences with an individual and learn that other people do not necessarily react toward them, feel toward them, or believe about them as they have come to think. This learning frees them to see themselves differently and to explore new ways of behaving and relating to others.

A helper working with abused children must react not to the child's immediate behavior but to the distorted expectations, fear, and rage the child is experiencing. The helper's reactions need to convey: "I'm not going to respond to you the way you have come to expect. I understand your fear and rage and I'm not going to hurt you with that knowledge." The child's experience with the helper should be: "I can't control this person with my strategies, but I'm safe anyway." This will permit the child to give up self-defeating strategies and explore new behaviors and relationships.

Discrimination. A second task for those working with abused children is to help the child understand his circumstances and discriminate between potentially abusive situations and the others he will encounter. It is important for the child to understand that while the abuse is not his fault, he has learned coping strategies (behaviors) to which people react with avoidance or rejection. It is important that the child come to recognize the distinction between himself as a person and his actions. This can be best accomplished by combining reassurances to the child that he is cared for with mild, nonphysical intervention with his behavior problems, including the guidance toward more useful, constructive ways to react.

Physical punishment and harsh criticism of a child's misbehavior is ineffective primarily because the child's maladaptive pattern is designed to respond to, cope with, and screen out this kind of criticism or verbal abuse. Using physical punishment with abused children is somewhat analogous to trying to put out a fire by throwing gasoline on it.

Alternatives. As indicated in the previous section, a child who has developed an essentially destructive pattern in response to the abusive experience needs to develop a variety of alternatives to cope with the stresses and problems he faces. Abused children have become uni-dimensional. They are inflexible and rigid. They tend to see things in black-and-white terms and do not know that there are alternatives to the way they behave. These alternatives must be taught. They must be modeled by people working with them.

At times, the child can be verbally guided into trying a new, more constructive reaction or behavior. If the results are favorable for the child, he will be encouraged to replace the destructive behavior with one more useful to him.

An example involves children who experience rejection from their peers due to their usually negative behavior. These children are frequently the butt of jokes and derision from other classmates because of their withdrawal and other maladaptive behaviors. They complain of being called names and they tend either to counter-attack with name-calling, which simply escalates the situation, or they withdraw into their hurt and disappointment. "Verbal judo" is a technique that has proved useful to children experiencing this problem. In "verbal judo" the child is instructed that when he is called a name, he is to reply by asking "What does that mean?" He is instructed, further, to repeat that same phrase regardless of the reply. This puts the name-callers off balance and creates some confusion for them. It has the effect of always leaving the ball in the court of the name-caller, and the most common outcome is for that person to slink away and avoid the embarrassment of that same situation in the future. Children have reported back to counselors with considerable glee, and with a sense of accomplishment and mastery in handling the situation without inviting further antagonism or feeling beat down and diminished.

Self-esteem. The fundamental way to encourage self-esteem in children is to listen respectfully to their feelings as they talk of their struggles with their lives. Children typically get this encouragement in their families, but it is generally absent in abusing families. Abused children have learned not to take risks by sharing with other people their fears, their hopes, their ideas, and their rage. In the context of a *safe* relationship, children inevitably begin to explore their feelings and perceptions, and if this exploration is met with interest and understanding, the child experiences a sense of worth and importance.

Mastery. Inherent in all of the above is developing within the child a sense of success. Children need to experience success in mastering some of their behavior problems. Basically, the child learns a sense of mastery, control, and worth through constructive achievement, in contrast to the destructive blocking and undermining that has been his only recourse in the past. In the same way that abuse and poor behavior feed on each other in a vicious cycle, confidence builds on success and success builds on confidence.

The following account is excerpted from the writing of a sophomore art student who was given the assignment to write a composition, "What Art Means to Me":

Art has become the center of my life. When I was younger, I thought of myself as completely worthless, incompetent, and ugly. In retrospect, this probably came out of my family life. My mother, who had had five marriages while I was living at home, was a heavy drinker and was always screaming at me about how worthless and ugly I was and how I had ruined her life. She blamed me for her husbands leaving her, and for a long time I thought it was probably true. One of them, a guy named Jerry, molested me. She said she didn't believe me when I told her about it, but I think that deep down she did, because after that she was always watching me, and they started having terrible fights with her accusing him of looking at other women.

I used to spend most of my time in my room and started drawing. I drew fantasy worlds where all people loved everyone and everyone was beautiful and kind. My seventh-grade art teacher encouraged me and told me I had talent. There wasn't anything I wouldn't do for her. My drawing, and later painting, became a place of safety for me. In the ninth grade I won a prize for a painting I did and it felt wonderful to feel like I had done something good. Since then, I have received recognition for my art work and also a scholarship. If it hadn't been for art, I would be either crazy or dead.

One of the most effective ways to help children is to

help the children's parents help them. Regardless of the terminology used, parents will be confronted by destructive coping strategies used by their children, including subversion, sabotage, cutting their losses, fading into the woodwork, and defensive interpretations. General antidotes to these classes of strategies were outlined earlier. The following table includes some samples of specific child behaviors under each of the defensive coping strategies—with examples of both effective and ineffective approaches to dealing with them.

Dealing with Child Problem Behaviors

Child Strategy/ Behavior Problem	Wrong (Ineffective) Approach	Correct (Effective) Approach
Subversion/sabotage: The child does the dishes as requested but sloppily leaves most dirty.	Complain about the child's poor attitude and do the dishes yourself.	Set up alternatives so that both parent and child can win—when you get the dishes clean you can watch television.
Creative stupidity: The child "forgets" how to do division.	Tell the child he/she is stupid and will never amount to anything if he/she doesn't learn math.	Have the parent review the steps in division and praise the child for the parts done correctly.
Cutting the losses: The child refuses to try to learn to ride a bike.	Tell the child that no one likes a person who won't try.	Have the parent show the child how to ride, giving whatever help is needed and praising the child's efforts.

Dealing with Child Problem Behaviors *(continued)*

Child Strategy/ Behavior Problem	Wrong (Ineffective) Approach	Correct (Effective) Approach
Fading into the woodwork: The child stays in his/her room and won't stay around the family.	Punish the child or tell him/her that no one likes people who act like that.	Have the parent arrange for family activities geared to the child's interests in which criticism and competition are forbidden.
Defensive interpretations: The child bursts into tears and angrily says, "You always blame me," when asked, "Who broke the lamp?"	Complain that the child always denies that it's his/her fault and point out past misbehaviors and mistakes.	Have the parent acknowledge the child's fear and upset and tell him/her that this time he just wanted to know how it happened.

6

Working with the Parents

To Whom It May Concern: Please help me. I think I am the worst mother in the world. I have three beautiful children, but I am messing up their lives so bad with my screaming at them and hitting them that I'm afraid they will never be OK and that they will never forgive me.

At night when I think about what I've done, I feel terrible. Sometimes I've thought of suicide but I know that wouldn't help my children.

I make promises that I will do better and be more patient and understanding, but when they make noise or knock something over or do anything, I just lose it.

My life is a disaster. I know I need help, but I'm so afraid that if I talk to someone, the state will take my children away. Maybe that would be better. It would be better for the kids, but I don't know if I could live through it.

I'm afraid I'm going to lose them anyway. How can children love a mother who does what I do? How can I stop? What is wrong with me? Please help me if you can.

—from a note brought by a mother to a counselor

One of the jobs in life for which preparation is the most haphazard is that of a parent. It is also the job for which there is little consensus regarding a job description. The bulk of our learning about being a parent is through being a child. Luckily for most people, those experiences plus love, dedication, and trial-and-error learning suffice. For others, however, the distorted views of parents and parenting learned in childhood become a block and a hindrance rather than a help in learning the job.

The axiom that abused children become abusing parents is mostly true. If we consider those people who were psychologically abused through constant disapproval, denigration, neglect, and verbal attacks, the axiom is even more true. Children are amazing in their resilience and ability to overcome abuse, poor parenting, and other traumas, and still turn out to be constructive human beings. If it were not for this resilience, the problem of abuse in our society would be much worse.

In the past it was fashionable to blame parents—especially mothers—for all of the problems of children, including mental illness, delinquency, school failure, behavior maladjustment, and possibly acne. More recently, the pendulum has swung and parents are being absolved of blame for many of these things, often through the shifting of blame to schools (or society in general), genetics, brain damage, and diet. There can, however, be no doubt that how children are raised (within broad limits) influences what kind of people they will become. Not all abused children will have problems as they grow up, but most will. Not all children raised in a loving, nurturing, stable home will develop into stable adults, but most will.

With rare exception, no parent sets out to abuse his or her children, and, in fact, abusing parents—even where the abuse has been severe—usually do not see themselves as abusing. They are simply responding in the only ways they can with ignorance, distress, and self-depreciation. Also, with rare exception, abusing parents love their children and do not intend them harm. The discrepancy in point of view about the abusing behavior held by abusing parents and outside observers is due to the parents' focusing on *their intentions* and the observer on the effects of the *parental behavior.*

While parents, like children, are as unique as finger-prints, there are common characteristics that abusing parents share in greater or lesser degrees, including social isolation, poor interpersonal skills, lack of self-esteem, ignorance about child-rearing methods, and the life stresses that come from financial, marital, and family problems. Abusing parents also tend to lack assertiveness skills and have problems with unresolved anger and resentment. Complex relationships between these characteristics result in vicious cycles that are difficult to break. For example, poor self-esteem leads people to permit others to exploit and degrade them, which in turn contributes to a disrespect for and discounting of oneself.

Martha, age twenty-nine and a school dropout, had four children from different fathers, none of whom married her. In talking about her traumatic personal history, Martha mentioned that she had been raped on two occasions: Therapist: "Tell me about the first time." Martha: "A neighbor man came over saying he wanted to borrow some coffee. When he got in the house, he started forcing me. I tried to fight him off at first, but my girls were asleep and I didn't want them to wake up and be scared, so after a while I just gave in." Therapist: "Tell me about the other time." Martha: "Later that day, he came back and did it again." It had not occurred to Martha that she had the right to call the police or take other measures to protect herself. It was part of the pattern of her discounting herself and seeing herself without value, worth, or rights.

Social Isolation. This usually includes one's estrangement from parents and family of origin, lack of peer relationships, and lack of success in sustaining a primary (spouse) relationship. The usual stresses encountered by all parents in coping with children's problems are overwhelming when there is no one with whom to share the burden. Non-isolated parents can get some relief from their daily struggles with their children by having friends and family provide respite child care, and can obtain some empathetic understanding by discussing their problems with these people. They can get self-validation in their relationships and obtain suggestions and support in their handling of problems with children. For isolated parents, the normal childhood problems and demands become overwhelming, not just a bad day or a difficult situation. Pretty twenty-two-year-old Janine, a single parent, says "I never know if what I am doing with the kids is right. Sometimes I resent them because I don't see how I can have friends because they take all my time—I never can meet a decent man, because they don't want to take on someone else's kids."

Poor Interpersonal Skills. These are at least first cousin to social isolation. Abusing parents often avoid social groups because they are unsure of themselves and do not know how to act. They often lack basic skills of making light conversation and are afraid of criticism and rejection. Many of these parents do not know how to interact with children apart from complaining, correcting, and punishing. Treatment programs for abusing parents should include elements of training in social and communication skills, how to play with children, and how to engage in recreational activities with their own families as well as others.

Lack of Self-esteem. This is an absence of that feeling of being worthy, capable, and valued. Poor self-esteem is both a cause and effect of abusive behavior. People with low self-esteem are people who dislike themselves and others similar to themselves; i.e., their children. They express this dislike by ignoring or rejecting the child and reacting destructively, and at times violently, to his misbehavior and demands. Parents dislike in their children traits they dislike in themselves, and where the self-dislike or -hate is pervasive, it leaves little room for appreciation of the child. The helplessness and self-disgust generated by the abusive behavior further damages any remaining shreds of self-worth.

Bryan, a young father who sought help after being frightened by his own behavior toward his three young children, reported, "When I hit the kids I feel terrible. I feel like a worthless piece of shit and I promise myself and God that I'll never do it again . . . but when they do what they do, I just can't help myself. I'm doing what my father did and I am afraid they will turn out like me."

Parents often look to their children to shore up their own flagging self-esteem. They look for approval from their children. Their children's misbehavior, failure to comply, and expressions of disagreement with the parent all become votes of no confidence or an assault on weak parental egos rather than merely misbehavior, noncompliance, or disagreement. Parents react with unrealistic anger when the child's actions become mixed with their own desperate need for reassurance. Joan, a thin, dark-haired mother said, "When Mark doesn't eat, it's like he is rejecting me. I try to be a good mother, but after going to the trouble to fix a good meal and he just picks . . . I've tried everything and nothing works."

Faulty Child-rearing. This can be both passive and active, consisting of both an absence of knowledge regarding child management and unrealistic expectations of children (in addition to faulty knowledge or beliefs). Typical unrealistic expectations are: believing that a three-year-old will happily share his toys or a four-year-old will be perfectly quiet because his dad is sleeping. Abusing parents generally expect children to like or agree with the directions and commands they give. Frequently, abusive episodes occur in situations in which a child complied with the parent's directive but did so begrudgingly or conveyed disagreement with the order.

In the words of Brad, a college student, while reminiscing about his troubled relationship with his abusive father: "I remember that as a kid my job was always to take out the garbage. I always did it, but my father would watch me and if I didn't look happy about it, or if I griped, he would start yelling and sometimes hit me—he called it disrespect. The rule of the garbage at home was: You had to take it out and you had to look like you enjoyed it."

Ignorance itself does not lead to abuse, but it traps the parent into ineffective reactions to children and sets impossibly high standards for the child and thereby for themselves. Ignorance is not bliss.

Life Stresses. If poor self-esteem, isolation, and ignorance are the gasoline in the abuse explosion, stress is the match. Most people experience financial, interpersonal, job, and other stresses, but non-abusing parents know that the problem will pass, and feel confident that they will somehow cope. Usually they have assurance that there are friends and family who will help. For abusing parents, on the other hand, the experience is: "I am in this alone, I don't know how to handle it, and it will be a perpetual disaster."

A tearful, thirty-year-old mother speaking from the witness chair at the trial of her husband, who was charged with assault of their ten-year-old son, said, "I know he loves our kids, but things got to be too much. He lost his job . . . we had bill collectors after us all the time . . . He wasn't sleeping and we were fighting most of the time. I think he just couldn't handle it, and he snapped. He has sometimes been too hard on the boy, but he has never done anything like this."

Non-assertiveness. Paradoxically, abusing parents are often the most passive and mild-mannered with people outside of the family. They tend to allow themselves to be exploited and pushed around. They store the anger and resentment generated by this exploitation and release it onto children, wives, and other more helpless beings. This process is called displacement: displacing anger generated by one source onto another person.

A young mother speaking to an evaluator about her husband, who had been accused of severely beating their infant daughter: "I just know he couldn't have done it. He is always so nice to everyone. He wouldn't hurt a fly. His parents are always demanding everything of him and they always put him down, but he never fights back. He just does the best he can to help them. He is just not a violent person."

7

The Parents' Coping Strategies

There is a children's toy called a Chinese Finger Puzzle. It is a small tube made of woven, flexible strips. If a person inserts his fingers into each end and then tries forcefully to pull them out, the puzzle clamps onto the fingers and, the harder a person pulls, the tighter the puzzle grips.

Everyone develops strategies for handling life stress. Fortunately, most of these work to some extent and do not have destructive side effects. In some cases, however, the strategies not only fail to help but they tend to exacerbate the problem. Coping strategies of this destructive type are often given such names, in psychological or psychiatric literature, as *repression, denial, displacement,* etc. Whatever the name, these patterns do not resolve the stress or problem, but rather serve to increase or perpetuate the problem.

Roger, a burly man with a large, dark beard, had been reported for abuse after slapping his eleven-year-old, leaving a large bruise. In talking about his anger, Roger reported, "I want my boy to love me. I know I have a temper and I try to control it. Whenever I correct him about something, he starts whining and crying. That makes me even madder, and I really lose it 'cause he's acting like I'm some kind of monster, child abuser, or something." His son, of course, is responding with fear to a history of being hurt in the wake of his father's anger.

Discounting. Parents who abuse their children over time are able to do so in part because they depersonalize, or "discount," the child and discount the impact of their abusive behavior on the child. It is incredible how a parent can talk about having only "swatted the child a few times" when the child has terribly bruised buttocks, back, and legs. While some abusive parents lie about their behavior, most of them actually believe that what they did was not so bad. A prerequisite to all kinds of abuse—physical and sexual—is parents' discounting or denying the consequences of their abuse of the child. There is an impaired ability to empathize with the child's experiences, resulting partly from the parents' absorption with their own needs and partly from being, themselves, frequently discounted by others.

Projection. This is one of the best-known and perhaps most overused defense mechanisms. It basically involves ascribing to others unworthy thoughts, motives, or deeds that are true of the person him/herself. In the context of abuse dynamics, it refers to the parent blaming the child for having made the parent behave in an abusive way.

Thirty-four-year-old Joleen, herself in the beginning stages of abusive behavior toward her two preschool daughters, talked about her own abused childhood:

It wasn't bad enough that my father would beat me with a belt until I was black-and-blue. Afterwards, he would spend hours talking to me about how I had made him do it and why did I treat him so bad? and why did I always do things I knew would make him mad? He would make me admit it was my fault, and then pray—sometimes it seemed like hours—that I would stop being so bad and that God would forgive me. I not only got to have the shit beat out of me, but then I would get to feel guilty about causing him so much hurt. It was confusing back then. Now I hate him for blaming me for what he did.

Projection enables a parent to continue abusive behavior with some feeling of justification. It is confusing for the child, of course, and generates self-hatred.

At times, parents project blame for their behavior on exculpating causes, such as substance abuse or even brain damage. In one case, the wife of a man who had repeatedly sexually abused his two stepdaughters and a natural daughter was a staunch defender and excuse maker for her husband. She initially blamed the girls for being provocative in their behavior and dress. When this did not "wash" with the counselor, at the next session she triumphantly announced that she had found the culprit: She had taken her husband to a chiropractor for a neck adjustment and, according to her story, a spinal dislocation had resulted in pressure being exerted on the man's brain. The pressure focused specifically on a brain center that caused incestuous behavior; apparently this was a "child-raping center." Parenthetically, the couple's daughters were ultimately permanently removed from the home because of the parents' intransigence.

Escalation. Where parents habitually respond to their children's misbehavior with physical punishment, they frequently adopt the faulty logic that "If some is good, more is better." If a parent assumes it is appropriate to hit the child for misbehavior, then when this doesn't work, he or she escalates the punishment in the belief that stronger measures will at length yield the desired results.

It has been demonstrated in research and everyday practical experiences that, while punishment can discourage some behavior, intense punishment blocks learning and results in a backlash of resentment and anger. In a situation where children fearfully anticipate being hurt, it is very difficult for them to concentrate on anything the parent is trying to teach them. Brad, a handsome, athletic college student, was at risk of failing college because of his inability to pass the basic math skills test. He had "mental block" regarding math which he attributed to experiences with an abusive father who "tutored" him in math during public-school years. His father would stand over Brad, impatiently explaining math concepts, and would hit him and scream at him when Brad did not understand or would make a mistake. "To this day whenever I have to do math I get anxious and break out in a sweat, and my mind goes blank."

8

Parent-Helping Strategies

A Spokane man who was once convicted of assaulting his 13-month-old daughter is sought by city police on a recent charge of fracturing the skull of his 12-day-old daughter, detectives said.

Henry _____, 28, is wanted on an arrest warrant charging him with second-degree assault. Officers have been unable to find him since the warrant was issued last week, police said.

He is accused of inflicting a skull fracture to Brandy, the daughter of Wendy _____, while babysitting the child April 12 at a residence at . . .

Detective Sheldon Reeve said this man is the child's father.

—Spokane Daily Chronicle, May 1988

A California man has been convicted of second-degree assault in an attack last year that left a young boy semi-comatose and bed-ridden with brain damage.

A King County Superior Court jury deliberated only 45 minutes Friday before convicting _____, 26, of Fresno. _____ was charged with beating _____ with a piece of 2-by-4, video cable and a belt.

Margaret Castle, director of nursing at the Sunshine Vista nursing home in Seattle, testified that she hopes _____, now 7, will be able to roll over in his bed and talk some day. The child is the son of _____'s girlfriend.

Prosecutors said they will ask Superior Court Judge Marsha Pechman to impose a harsh penalty against _____, possibly as long as 10 years in prison, when he is sentenced July 18.

"Everybody is looking at me like I'm a monster or something." _____testified Friday. "I'm not . . . I tried to be a good father." "I never thought nothing like this would happen," he said. "I went through it. I survived. . . . Now I know it was wrong."

The boy was taken to a hospital on December 4. He suffered two broken arms that had been left untreated for about seven weeks.

—Spokesman-Review Spokane Chronicle, June 1988

Everyone has read media accounts of appalling instances of child abuse, instances in which children have been maimed or killed. Our natural reaction is sorrow for the child and outrage at the parent. We imagine the parent as a slobbering, ugly, subhuman, sadistic beast. We assuage our outrage by imagining and talking about different kinds of medieval punishment for the parent and expect at least long-term imprisonment, if not capital punishment, for this monster. We do this in part to distance ourselves from these "abusers" and ignore the fact that there are more similarities between *us* and *them* than there are differences.

This reaction is also a hindrance to us in working with abusing parents. Greg, a dedicated young mental health worker, after his first meeting in a treatment session with a group of abusing parents, reported to his supervisor, "I don't know if I can work with these people. When I think about what they have done to their children, I get sick to my stomach. I feel angry—I'm sure it must show."

This kind of abhorrence and anger at abusing parents is an indulgence that we cannot afford if we care about the long-range consequences to the children. As stated earlier: "It is difficult, if not impossible, to salvage the children without the parents."

Empathy with the Parent. To work successfully with abusing parents, these natural negative reactions to them, as well as the complications presented by the legal system, must be overcome. Empathy is needed for the parents' position, as is hope that they can do better when given better tools, knowledge, and relief from stress.

Aligning with the parents is more possible if we get to know them. Knowing the pain, confusion, and trauma that they have experienced, while not justifying their abusive behavior, at least makes it more understandable. Seeing the need and love the children have for their parents, despite the abuse they have experienced, makes our efforts at helping effect a reconciliation worthwhile.

James, a nine-year-old, freckle-faced boy who could be cast as Huckleberry Finn, said with tears in his eyes, "I miss my mom and dad. Joe and Linda [foster parents] are nice to me, but it's not the same as being at home. I just want to go home."

Baby Steps. A well-known talk show psychologist emphasized "baby steps" to her callers. That is, she conveyed to people that the focus of change of habits or behavior patterns occurs only in small, discrete steps. If a worker has an assignment of moving (by hand) a two-ton pallet of bricks to a location 100 yards away, he will exhaust himself and get a hernia pushing against the whole pallet. He will eventually get the job done only by moving a few bricks at a time. In the same way, if people believe that everything has to be done immediately, they will become discouraged, give up, and come away with yet another defeat and reason for self-recrimination and lack of confidence.

If a parent's problem constellation includes lack of assertiveness, poor child-management skills, poor self-esteem, overwhelming financial stress, and social isolation, these problems have to be broken into small parts and handled piece by piece. Marie, a young mother, had been dominated all her life by her own parents, who were critical of most things she did, including her housekeeping. They seemed insensitive to the fact that she had three active children between the ages of one and five. With encouragement from a counselor, she told her parents, in the middle of their criticism toward her about the condition of her home, "I am sorry you don't approve of my housekeeping. It is more important to me that I spend time with the kids than keeping everything neat. I feel okay about how I am doing." Despite her parents' unhappiness with her response, and their threat to stay away, she was elated at having stood up to them and her self-respect increased by a small increment. This also diminished her fear that something terrible would happen if she stood her ground with her parents.

Alternatives. To change what they are doing, people have to recognize that their behavior is wrong, ineffective, or destructive. It is equally true that, in order to change, people must be aware of alternatives and have some hope that these alternatives are accessible to them. Fortunately, abusing parents are like other people in that, fundamentally, they want the same things: They want to be good parents; they want to be accepted, respected, and successful, and to be free from self-doubt, fear, and confusion. To the extent that these basic motives can be tapped and then directed to "power" changes, these people can be helped.

In the same way that children are trapped by their limited awareness of alternative ways of reacting or behaving, so too are parents trapped by their restricted range of response to their children's needs and behaviors. In the words of one particularly insightless and difficult parent: "I yell at 'em and if that don't work, I hit 'em and if that don't work, I hit 'em harder. It worked with me when I was a kid and it'll work with my kids."

Luckily, most parents want to parent effectively and,

given appropriate guidance, will substitute workable responses and solutions for ineffective ones. They will respond to guidance and suggestions presented without blame or recrimination. In most cases, parents are already experiencing overwhelming feelings of inadequacy and self-disgust, so that disapproval from a helping person is redundant and counterproductive.

Assertiveness. As discussed earlier, one of the common problems of abusing parents is their inability to be appropriately assertive. Nonassertiveness results in ineffectual handling of stress, difficulties, and disappointments and creates that reservoir of resentment and anger that is frequently displaced onto children. It also helps perpetuate the chronic poor self-esteem that is so common with abusing parents. Helping parents to develop assertiveness requires that they be given concrete specific guidance and be encouraged to use "baby steps" to become more self-affirming and assertive. Parents should be encouraged to stand up for themselves through self-affirming statements and behavior.

Cynthia, a gentle, pretty, good-natured wife and mother, sought help for chronic depression. Her depression was mainly "situational"—caused by her life circumstances: primarily an abusive, philandering, controlling husband. He kept her on an inadequate budget while spending money on recreational vehicles, sports equipment, and other adult toys. He constantly criticized her for her appearance and weight, although by normal standards she was an unusually attractive woman. He paid scant attention to the children and openly flaunted his affairs. Cynthia admitted with guilty tears that she was becoming harsh with the children, screaming at them and "spanking them too hard."

Cynthia's position was one of long-suffering patience. She desperately feared being alone. She believed that it would be unfair to her children to leave her husband—

because they "needed a father." She saw herself as incompetent and was afraid she could not manage if she were alone. She was also a religious person, whose upbringing taught her that wives should "submit to their husbands" and that divorce was contrary to God's will. After months of struggling with these issues, the therapist, partly in desperation, said, "You know, Cynthia, the meek shall inherit the earth . . . after everyone else is through with it." This stuck with Cynthia. Soon thereafter, she screwed up her courage and threw her husband out. Within a short time he returned, hat in hand, asking to come back and promising to reform. Her decision about accepting him back is less important than the fact that this self-affirming action gave her a new sense of self-esteem, confidence, and self-respect.

One psychologist uses what he calls the "dog turd gimmick" in working with people who are pathologically nonassertive. A wadded Kleenex is offered to the client with the statement "I want to give you something, this is a dog turd." Nonassertive people always accept the "gift," usually with a puzzled look. The psychologist then retrieves the Kleenex and repeats the offer and statement to the client for as many times as it takes the client to finally refuse to accept the offer. The record is twenty-two repeats. The point of this game is to help the person perceive, in a direct way, that he/she is accepting others' disparagement and, more important, that he/she need not do so.

Child-care Skills. If lack of knowledge about how to care for, or "manage," children were the primary cause of child abuse, the whole problem would be far more easily resolved. It unfortunately isn't. Poor skills, distorted attitudes, emotional problems, and situational factors such as stress combine to precipitate child abuse. These factors constitute a tangled fish line of reciprocal problems in which each exacerbates or solidifies the next. As in untangling a fish line, it is important to begin with that part of the knot that is available to be unraveled. Specific child-care skills often fit this bill. In addition, unraveling one part frees up other parts that are not initially accessible. Psychologists have long noted that behavioral changes result in positive changes in attitudes as well as in feelings of well-being.

People commonly focus on changing attitudes initially, with the (not unrealistic) hope that such changes will result in behavioral changes. However, it is often easier to initiate changes in *behavior*, which will just as surely result in *attitude* change. Salesmen have long recognized this principle in sales approaches. If they can get people to *act* as if they own something, usually they make a sale. The fact is, the relationship between attitudes and behavior is reciprocal. Each influences and shapes the other.

Finally, dealing with people about specific skills and knowledge is usually less threatening than is focusing on attitudes and emotional problems.

Joan, a thirty-one-year-old, dark-haired wife and mother, has been referred for counseling because of repeated incidents of abusive punishment of Mark, her eight-year-old son. Talking to members of the family, made it apparent that most of the abusive episodes occurred around mealtimes. Joan would prepare a meal, knowing from past experience that Mark would pick at the food and not eat. Mark revealed that he was aware of the history of conflict and abuse around mealtimes and that he approached meals with trepidation and anxiety that eliminated any appetite. Mark made feeble efforts to eat, but, experiencing his mother's mounting frustration and anger, would be unable to continue. The episodes typically ended in another incident of abuse (verbal or physical) with an aftermath of anger, hurt, and recrimination. Not surprisingly, Joan herself had grown up in an abusive home, had poor self-esteem, and was nonassertive.

The therapist assured Joan that Mark's behavior was indeed a significant problem and it was understandable that any good parent would be concerned about a child's not eating. Joan was then instructed to place a meal in front of Mark and set a timer to go off in thirty minutes. She was further instructued to leave the area where Mark was eating and, upon hearing the timer, to return and remove the meal, informing Mark that his next opportunity to eat would come at the next regularly scheduled meal. This gave Joan a specific "consequence" to administer for her child's not eating—removal of the meal, with no snacks until the next meal—as a substitute for abuse. It also reduced Joan's exposure to the implied accusation of being a bad parent when Mark would not eat. In Joan's mind, the refusal of her son to eat was rejection of both her nurturing and her as a parent. More important, Mark no longer had to confront his mother's anger and anticipate abuse during mealtimes.

Mark ate now, once his appetite was not impaired by fear. Joan gained an immediate sense of accomplishment with him. This increased her self-respect by at least a small increment and gave her hope that the problem could be solved. The same pattern was subsequently extended to other, at times more difficult, problem situations, and with each small success, Joan's feeling of competency and worth increased. At the same time, Mark's feelings of trust increased and his general level of anxiety declined.

While there are a large number of parent skills and a variety of ways of describing them, the following list is one that practical experience suggests constitutes worthwhile and understandable approaches for parents:

1. *Punish the act, not the child.* This hoary concept deserves emphasis. In practical terms, it means focusing on what the child did—not what the child is. Comments such as "You are stupid," "You are clumsy," "You don't care about

anybody but yourself," "You are inconsiderate," etc., are all attacks on·the child. Comments such as "You didn't do what I told you," "You broke the lamp," "You hurt your sister," etc., focus on the behavior.

Parents often mistakenly believe that the tone and/or volume of voice is most important and that using a soft, sweet voice with polite phrases will produce desired results. The fact is that, while their refraining from shouting or screaming helps, it is the words themselves that either direct or wound. Saying to a child softly, "Dear, you are a selfish, stupid, inconsiderate slob," will devastate and tear down a child's self-worth. Yelling angrily, "I am furious that you came in late and haven't done any of your chores," may or may not be effective, but it will not damage the child.

2. *Use natural consequences.* The closer the consequence matches the misbehavior, the greater the potential for learning. Ultimately, children should grow up behaving correctly or appropriately because to do otherwise frustrates their own goals or causes them problems. Artificial or irrelevant consequences may inhibit a particular misbehavior but run the risk of creating resentment, which leads to power struggles and does nothing to promote mature, responsible behavior.

Mary, an anxious, gangly eleven-year-old, was in counseling for peer and school problems. Part of her problem concerned her mother, who was unusually harsh and demanding, to the point of being (at least, psychologically) abusive. The mother insisted that Mary and her nine-year-old sister not snack after school until obtaining permission from her after she returned home from work. Such requests were seldom granted. The mother set out a heaping dish of M&M's candy in plain sight and ordered the children not to touch it. The girls tried to take pieces of the candy from the dish in ways that they hoped would not be missed. Eventually, the whole stack was undermined and collapsed, making their thefts obvious.

As punishment for this infraction, the mother required that Mary (who, being oldest, was held responsible) write, 500 times, "I will not take food without asking permission from Mother." The mother further stipulated that if the child did not finish these 500 sentences within the time available after school, another 500 would be added. By the time of the next counseling session with Mary, she was desperate and in tears, still having left to write about 1400 sentences. When asked what the sentence was that she had to write, Mary replied, "I can't remember." She had reverted to writing the sentences in columns by first filling up a column of "I's," second a column of "will's," etc. Apart from the severity of the punishment (the consequence), it was ineffective because it had no "natural" relationship to the offense.

3. *Use punishment sparingly and in mild forms.* The primary value of punishment is information. The information conveyed through punishment is that a particular act or behavior should not be done. Punishment does not provide information to the child on what *should be done in its place.* At times, the primary goal is to stop the particular behavior rather than teach a new one.

Punishment is appropriate in situations where the child's behavior puts himself or other people in immediate risk, including such things as riding their trikes in the street, running across intersections without regard for traffic or lights, playing with knives, matches, and other dangerous things, etc. Punishment inevitably creates a certain amount of fear and anger. Fear and anger are not beneficial in the child management or teaching process. They are, in fact, undesirable side effects. Where anger and fear are too intense, they destroy learning and contribute to the cycle of misbehavior and negative reactions that forms part of the cycle of abuse.

Punishment is in some respects like medication. All medication has certain undesirable side effects, and in using the medication the practitioner strives to find a dosage level that maximizes the positive benefits and minimizes the negative side effects. The strength of the dose of punishment used should have this same goal: that is, to ensure that the amount of information conveyed by the punishment is greater than the negative side effects of fear and anger. In the case of Mary in the candy caper cited earlier, the mother's punishment was so extreme that the child simply invested her energy into finding ways of circumventing the punishment rather than learning anything from the experience.

4. *Accentuate the positive.* This song title from the children's classic movie *Song of the South* embodies the wisdom of the ages. Accentuating the positive in this context means to pay attention to, acknowledge, and reward the child's positive, or good, behaviors. It is not just a matter of being nice. There is a sound, practical basis for accentuating the positive: Rewarding or acknowledging good behavior conveys more information to the child than punishing a bad act.

Rewarding good behavior, or any reasonable approximation of good behavior, on the part of a child tells the child what will please the parent or be acceptable. Punishment tells him or her what is not acceptable but does not tell what, out of an infinite array of alternatives, is acceptable. Rewarding the child for *approximations* to acceptable behavior serves as a beacon light to direct the child to acceptable behavior. At least as important as the communication aspect of accentuating the positive is the fact that a child who experiences rewards or approval tends to respect and like himself, as well as the parent. This factor by itself promotes a more positive attitude on the part of the child. Children raised on a diet of criticism, punishment, or disapproval become angry, anxious children who are constricted and afraid to explore and grow.

Two young children, ages nine and seven, decided while their parents were away to surprise them by making bread.

They had watched their mother make bread and were aware that they needed to mix flour and a few other ingredients. They used about half a sack of flour and water but after finding that the mass was too sticky, again added flour and in their attempts to balance the amount eventually used the whole sack and had to move the mess into a sink as the only container large enough to hold it. At the time the parents returned home, the children were still desperately trying to balance the water and flour and had pretty much devastated the kitchen.

The parents, in this instance, recognizing that the intention of the children was to do something worthwhile or positive, were able to refrain from what was their initial reaction of anger and upset, and simply helped the children clean up the kitchen and subsequently start a new batch of bread, helping them learn how to make bread. What could have been a devastating experience for these children became a learning experience. The children knew they had done wrong and did not need additional information about that. They needed to know what to *do*—in this case, the correct way to make bread.

5. *Bonding is the basis of obedience.* Children obey their parents largely because they do not want to displease them, not because they are afraid of being punished. This is not to say that children do not fear punishment—because they do. But the bulk of the fear is the fear of the loss of their parents' esteem and love. In order for children to fear the loss of parental love and esteem, they first have to feel that they have it. This bond of mutual love and esteem is forged through a history of shared, positive experiences. It is built from experiences that a child has with a parent where the child feels good about himself and feels trusting of the parent. Regardless of how skillful the parent is with discipline, natural consequences, nutrition, housekeeping, or any other parental task, raising children will be a laborious and joyless duty

without the foundation glue of bonding (mutual attachment) and caring.

Parents should ensure that they spend time with their children when the only purpose is to enjoy the child and allow the child to enjoy the parents. Where parents have multiple children, they would do well to spend time alone with each child, even if only occasionally and even if in doing so it reduces the total amount of "family togetherness" time. For some parents who themselves have never had the experience of being nurtured and cared about as children, who in effect have never been children themselves, these tasks of bonding with their own children will be difficult. They need special help and guidance in accomplishing them.

It is beyond the scope of this book to outline all of the possible approaches to working with parents and bonding issues, but some of these approaches include:

(a) Coaching the parent during periods of parent/child interaction to learn their children's signals for seeking attention and approval and to learn how to respond to the children's approaches and interact with them. Many parents, for example, not only don't know how to play with their children, but it has not occurred to them that playing with their children is either desirable or possible.

(b) Helping the parents talk about their own needs as children so that they make the connection between their own experiences and their children's current needs.

(c) Encouraging parents to express their own needs for nurturing and allow themselves to be nurtured and cared for by partner or family members. People who have permission to seek and enjoy nurturing or caretaking for themselves can better permit and respond to the same in their own children.

6. *Uncluttered communication.* Human communication is in-

credibly complex. It is amazing not that messages between people get confused, but that communication is as effective as it seems to be. The meaning of a message is defined by the actual meaning of the words (lexicon), the context or situation in which the communication occurs, and paralingual cues (voice inflections, body gestures, facial expressions).

Communication is further complicated since the variety of channels of communication (word meanings, gestures, etc.) may be used to convey different or even conflicting messages at the same time. A young woman alone at a bus stop at night, approached by a leering unknown male who asks, "Do you have the time?" will interpret the message far differently than if she is at work, rushing to finish a project with a co-worker who asks exactly the same question.

Parents are frequently very confusing in their communications to children. They *ask questions* when they mean to *give directions* or *make demands.* Questions to a four-year-old, such as "Would you like to go to bed now?" or "Do you really want to hit Mommy?" may sound polite but are potentially confusing to the child. Parental directives should be stated emphatically and directly such as: "I want you to go to bed" or "Do not hit me" or "Do not flush the cat down the toilet." It also helps to get all of the child's communication channels focused by making eye contact with the child and holding the child gently by the shoulders while giving the directive. To ensure that an important directive or message is received, it is a good idea to take a page out of the book of professional communicators, such as radio operators, and have the child repeat back the message. Doing so ensures that the message sent is the message received, and provides an opportunity to correct any message distortions.

Working with abusing parents is a complex and at times draining process. A balance must be maintained between reassuring and supporting the parents while moving the parents toward changes in their parenting behavior. The parents' defensiveness must be confronted while maintaining support with them, and all of this needs to be done while maintaining the goal of assuring the well-being and safety of the child or children. Work with each parent or set of parents requires an individualized, tailored approach that takes into account the array of parent and child problems and needs.

The following table provides samples of ineffective and effective ways of dealing with the typical destructive parent coping strategies.

Dealing with Parent Coping Strategies

Destructive Coping Strategies	Wrong (Ineffective) Approaches	Correct (Effective) Approaches
Discounting/disregarding the child's needs, feelings, etc. Minimizing impact on the child of abusive behavior.	Point out the parent's lack of empathy and the destructiveness of his/her approach.	"Active listen" to the parent's needs, etc. Point out cues to the child's feelings and experiences.
Projection: ascribing to the child bad intent or motives for his/her misbehavior.	Tell the parent he/she is projecting and point out how wrong he/she is about the child.	Focus on "legitimate" concerns the parent has about the child's behavior. Make suggestions for handling the problem behavior.
Escalation: using increasingly severe forms of punishment; e.g., spankings.	Express outrage and disgust with the parent's excesses. Point out how abusive the parent has been.	Provide the parent with effective substitute approaches to child management.

Destructive Coping Strategies	Wrong (Ineffective) Approaches	Correct (Effective) Approaches
Displacement: The parent acts out anger and resentment (derived from other sources) against the child.	Tell the parent that his/her approach is wrong and that children don't deserve such treatment.	Help the parent to be more assertive and teach him/her to confront the real sources of his/her frustration and anger.
Repression/denial: The parent hides or refuses to acknowledge his/her destructive behavior or its effects on the child.	Provide evidence, definitions, etc., that the parent is being destructive and abusive.	Reassure the parent as regards the positive aspects of his/her parenting. Focus on solving the problem. Express understanding of the parent's frustrations.

9

Therapy with Children

T herapy is a peculiar relationship between two or more people. It is a relationship that is at the same time artificial and intimate. It has more or less explicit sets of rules of behavior, expectations, and designated roles. One or more people are designated "helper" (therapist, counselor, doctor) and one or more are designated "helpee" (patient, client, consumer). There are many therapeutic frameworks used by therapists. Except for a relatively small number of purists who adhere closely to one "school" or another, therapists are eclectic, having forged an amalgamated system out of their own experiences along with their training in one or more of the formal systems of therapy.

There are a variety of ways of organizing and classifying the array of therapy approaches used, but all of them focus to some extent on a client's or patient's thinking, behavior, or emotions. Some focus largely on *thinking processes* that include self-perceptions, interpretations of past problems and other events, and predictions about others' behavior. These "cognitive" therapies attempt to help people develop more realistic and functional understandings about themselves and others.

Therapists who focus on *emotions or feelings* work on helping people to express feelings effectively and managing them. At times, they encourage catharsis (venting of feelings) and focus on helping people to develop the ability to experience their feelings accurately and constructively.

Therapists who focus on the *behavior* of a client use a variety of approaches to get people to behave differently. These can range from managing the contingencies of reinforcement (rewards, or in some cases punishment) to role playing or the practice of behaviors.

All of these therapeutic approaches are legitimate and are useful for people, depending on the skill of therapist and the quality of participation taken by the client or patient.

There is an underlying unity among all therapy approaches because feeling, thinking, and behaving are all part and parcel of the same entity. How we think affects how we behave and feel, how we feel affects how we behave and think, and just as surely how we behave shapes how we think and feel. The choice of therapy approach is most often dictated by which system—thinking, feeling, behaving—is most accessible, and by the theoretical leaning of the therapist.

It is impossible to discuss therapy without making assumptions about how people "tick," including what drives them (motivation), how they learn, and the nature of their disordered or dysfunctional responses. Learning refers to the acquisition of understanding, skills, and habit patterns. Deviant, disturbed, or dysfunctional responses include behavioral, cognitive, and emotional components. The following assumptions are as good as any, without becoming too technical:

Motivation. People are motivated or driven to experience positive feelings, understand their environment, grow and develop in terms of competency, be safe from pain or fear, experience approval, have connections with others, and be stimulated. Conversely, people are motivated to avoid unpleasant feelings such as confusion, disapproval, isolation, boredom, and injury or hurt.

Learning. People learn; that is, they acquire patterns of thought, feeling, and behaving that (first of all) are available to them through their trial-and-error experiences and other teaching and (second) that maximize positive experiences and minimize negative ones. Learning is enhanced by direct experience, although as children acquire language they can learn symbolically, through teaching and modeling, by and from people around them.

Dysfunctional Patterns. Every human being experiences fear or anxiety, failure, frustration, and sadness. These are part of the business and price of being human. Fear and failure are not in themselves debilitating, nor do they constitute mental or emotional problems or psychological dysfunction. Dysfunctional behavior consists of patterns of perception, emotion, and action that exacerbate or perpetuate the distress, pain, or fear that the child is trying to reduce or eliminate. Apart from chemical or neurologically based abnormalities—such as schizophrenia, organic brain syndrome, and bipolar disorders (manic-depressive illness)—all dysfunctional behavior patterns are characterized by this kind of circularity.

For example, shyness is basically an anticipation of rejection by others. Behaving shyly (social withdrawal, avoiding eye contact, not initiating conversations with others, etc.) results in exactly the rejection or discounting that the shy person fears. The pattern of poor self-esteem, anticipation of failure, withdrawal and consequent poor response from others further exacerbates the feelings of unworthiness and sense of failure that characterize the dilemma of many abusive parents and abused children. The therapist's task is to break the cycle by changing the perception, the feeling, or the behaving so that the basic needs are met (at least for the most part) and in a way that does not perpetuate the original pain or fear.

As stated earlier, any therapeutic approach is embedded, intentionally or otherwise, in a system of beliefs about how people operate: what makes people "tick," how they learn, and what constitutes dysfunction. In the case of abused children, and in the system presented here, there are four basic assumptions:

(a) The abused child's dysfunctional pattern results from the distorting experiences of the abuse situation.

(b) The pattern of behavior, however dysfunctional it appears, was reasonable and natural given the child's experiences and available options.

(c) The basic intention of the child (original motivation) for the dysfunctional pattern is legitimate; i.e., somewhere imbedded in the behavior pattern is a legitimate, worthy need or intention. Generally, the intention or need is to avoid further fear, pain, and depreciation.

(d) If the child has the opportunity to experience an alternative that both fulfills the basic legitimate need and avoids the negative by-product of exacerbating or perpetuating the problem, he or she will acquire the new functional pattern and give up the dysfunctional one.

Conceptually, it has been useful to diagram the interaction as follows:

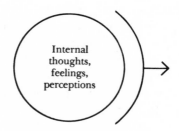

Internal thoughts, feelings, perceptions

The shield and arrow imply that the dysfunctional pattern is designed both to protect (shield) the child from a social environment (e.g., abuse) and to structure (arrow) the environment to make it safer and less painful.

An example would be Max, a child who experienced considerable psychological abuse (consistent blame, name-calling, and rejection) along with occasional abuse that was physical. Max was failing in school because, fearing ridicule and criticism, he spent his time in class daydreaming, and was afraid to try. He dealt with other people primarily by withdrawal and a refusal to interact, even refusing to talk or respond to questions. Max used the same approach, of course, when confronted with a therapist. Schematically, the interaction would be diagramed as follows:

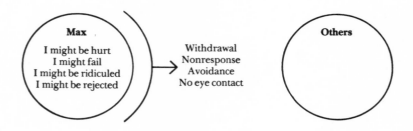

Inevitably, as Max used his defense system with people, they reacted to Max—if not sooner, then later—with puzzlement, irritation, and eventually by discounting and ignoring him. While these responses from people were not satisfying and certainly did not meet Max's needs for validation and acceptance, they were better than his worst fears of criticism, rejection, and abuse.

The task for the therapist in working with Max was to avoid reaffirming the dysfunctional pattern and to help him experience an alternative way of relating to others that would be more generally useful and successful. Any direct response to his being noncommunicative would run the risk of appearing to Max as some kind of an attack on him. This would include statements (however well-meaning) such as "Why don't you want to talk?", "How about talking to me?", "People won't like you if you don't talk to them," "What's the matter, cat got your tongue?"

Under the system being presented, responses from the therapist that qualify as "therapeutic" would be directed toward the needs, intentions, or internal feelings that Max is experiencing. These would include such things as "I wonder if you get lonely" and "I guess I wouldn't talk if I thought people would jump on me for what I said." This would be diagramed as follows:

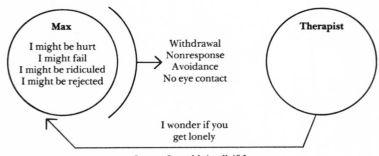

When done correctly, the "therapeutic response" has the effect of bypassing, and thereby invalidating or neutralizing, the defensive behavior and giving the child an experience with safety and acceptance, along with an opportunity for him to explore his pain. None of this is to imply that a given response or effort by a therapist is always accurate, or that when it is accurate it undoes the years that it has taken the child to develop the defensive response pattern. However, a consistent series of therapeutic communications can undo this damage and enable the child to give up a disturbed pattern for a healthy one. More important, it allows the child to behave in ways that elicit from others the healing balm of acceptance, understanding, and validation.

In the particular case of Max, the initial meeting with him occurred in the context of a family session, including along with Max his single mother and two older siblings, a brother and a sister. Max seated himself as far from the therapist and other family members as possible, ducked his head into his coat, and stared at his hands. The mother and brother and sister immediately began to criticize him and offer examples of Max's failures and lack of responsiveness. The therapist interrupted this by taking Max gently by the hand and leading him to a seat next to him with the comment, "It looks like you need someone to be on your side." The therapist then commented that Max seemed to have made a promise to himself that he was not going to talk and that the "rest of us" needed to respect that. He said further that Max should keep the promise of not talking, but that the rest of the group would go ahead and have a discussion.

As the discussion progressed, focusing on the frustration that the mother was experiencing trying to balance home responsibilities with work, etc., Max began to write furiously with materials available on a desk next to where he was seated and eventually gave the notes to his mother to read. His notes included comments regarding his perceptions of the family problems, and the therapist and other family members agreed that writing comments did not break his "vow of silence."

While the actual events were more complicated than the scenario described above, they had the elements of avoiding attacking Max's defense structure by acknowledging and encouraging the boy to keep his promise. At the same time, Max was validated by the therapist's verbal and nonverbal siding with him. In subsequent sessions, Max elected to talk to the therapist directly since, we can assume, writing was more laborious, his communicating (in writing) did not result in criticism, and the silent approach wasn't working in any case.

While the basic approach is to interact with the child by speaking to the feelings, thoughts, intentions, and needs that constitute the core of his/her dilemma in a way that bypasses the defense system, there are a number of therapeutic approaches or techniques that are useful in working with children. Some of them are only available after the child has developed some trust in the therapist and has, more or less, started to give up the defenses.

Reflective Listening. This is a widely understood and used technique that can be powerful in working with children. It is used both to help in discovering or understanding basic dilemmas experienced by the child as well as in conveying to the child caring interest and validation. It contributes something both to the child's perception that the therapist hears what is being said and to his feeling of being worthy and important. The range of reflecting can involve simple restatements of the child's words, up to reading between the lines in an attempt to understand the needs, intentions, feelings, etc., being experienced internally. Reflective listening is nonjudgmental and noncritical, with only the goal of understanding the child. The following table provides examples of reflective statements ranging from simple acknowledgment to "reading between the lines":

A child says	Simple acknowledgment	Reading between the lines
All the kids are jerks.	The kids at school are jerks.	The kids at school treat you bad.
My parents don't lis- to me.	You don't feel like your parents hear what you say.	You are afraid your parents aren't interested in what you say.
I'm going to kill Jerry.	You are really mad at Jerry.	Jerry has done something that has hurt you a lot.
Counseling is stupid.	You think counseling is a waste of time.	I think you're afraid I might hurt you.

Catharsis. This is another widely used and understood technique that basically constitutes the expressing of feelings—usually intense and negative feelings. The value of catharsis is that it temporarily relieves pressure and, in doing so, can enable the child to work more effectively with the problems confronting him. It does not solve problems in and of themselves. It has an additional positive effect of conveying to the child that his or her feelings are legitimate. Generally, it should be followed up on by work on how to handle the situations that are the focus and cause of the feelings.

Catharsis with children can be accomplished in a variety of ways, ranging from direct to indirect. A direct way would be to permit or encourage the child to fantasize about ways of "getting even" with people who have hurt him.

Amy, a freckle-faced seven-year-old, for example, gleefully talked about taking Jim (an abusive boyfriend of her mother) and dropping him out of an airplane and then dropping bombs on him. She said 100-pound bombs, the therapist suggested 1,000-pound bombs, and she countered with 1,000,000-pound bombs. It is important that the child understand that this is only pretend and be clear that these are not acceptable, real solutions. Parenthetically, the more outrageous or outlandish the fantasies, the less likely they will be taken seriously. Fantasy catharsis should be followed by some kind of input or decision about real ways of handling the situation. For example, the therapist and Amy agreed that the best plan was for Amy to stay away from Jim.

Catharsis can be accomplished through other means, such as art work, throwing darts (preferably the Velcro type, without sharp points), storytelling, and pillow pounding or some other sort of physical pounding with Batacas (foam rubber bats) or other such devices.

Role Playing. Especially with latency age or younger children, role playing can be an effective way both for the child to convey his or her fears, resentments, and conflicts and to explore alternative approaches and solutions for the problem(s). Younger children are less self-conscious and enter into role playing easier than adolescents. In fact, younger children frequently initiate role playing through play activities where appropriate materials are available, such as dollhouses, dolls, cars, sandboxes, etc.

The following exchange between Charlene, a rather quiet, pretty, black six-year-old, and her therapist occurred following her disclosure that her stepfather had burned her on the back with a cigarette because she wet the bed:

CHARLENE carefully arranged a dollhouse and a sand tray, and started pouring sand on the house.

THERAPIST: It looks like we have to have sand on the house.

CHARLENE (*pouring more sand*): Yes, it's burning.

THERAPIST: How did the fire start?

CHARLENE: I started it to burn up the baby.

THERAPIST (*effecting the high voice of a baby*): Oh, the house is burning. Why did you start the house on fire?

CHARLENE (*effecting a gravelly, low voice*): Because you keep wetting the bed.

THERAPIST: But I can't help it, I'm just a kid.

CHARLENE: You're old enough to not wet the bed.

THERAPIST: But I'm still learning and sometimes I have accidents.

CHARLENE: Well, you shouldn't have done it.

THERAPIST: But you should never burn children.

CHARLENE *(after a long pause):* But what if they are bad?

THERAPIST: It doesn't matter. Children should never be burned.

CHARLENE: Then what should we do?

THERAPIST: Let's put the fire out and promise never to burn anyone. If they do something bad, we will just help them to stop doing it.

CHARLENE: Is the baby okay?

THERAPIST: Well, she got burned a little, but she will be okay.

The essential message in this brief exchange was that the child (Charlene herself in this case) did not deserve to be burnt and hurt, even if she did something wrong. One of the first steps in helping abused children is to relieve them from blaming themselves for being hurt.

An example that includes elements of both role playing and catharsis has been developed by intuitive and skilled therapists working in a child abuse project at the Spokane Community Mental Health Center. It is called the "elephant nest" and is used with pre-latency aged children (about ages four to eight) who have had to deal with not only the grinding trauma of serial abuse and neglect, but also the trauma of being removed from their homes and placed with foster families. Placement in foster homes for these children is usually traumatic, regardless of the degree of abuse and neglect they have experienced in their own homes. The "elephant nest" technique involves use of a variety of media, including painting, chalk or marker board, flannel board, doll play, role playing, puppets, and clay.

The story begins with a family of birds—representing the child and his original birth family—who live in a nest. A series of traumatic events follows (representing the abuse, removal from the home, and family upset). The baby birds are then removed from the fractured nest and taken to a foster elephant and placed in a basket on the elephant's back. The elephant is a benign creature who cares for the baby birds after the nest comes apart and the baby birds are removed from the parent nest.

As the children develop and play at these scenarios of the parent birds' allowing the nest to fall apart, the children express their ambivalence toward the elephant, who provides caretaking, as well as toward the parent birds. They express the wish that the fractured nest be healed. They express their anger at the parents for not mending the nest and other intense feelings that are both diagnostic of the children's problems and offer opportunities for the therapist to understand and help the children understand what is happening to them in their lives. The story provides understanding of, and help with, the child's moving through the trauma stages of panic or alarm, intense anger or loss, despair, and integration.

Finding the Valid Intent. This is probably more a direction as opposed to a technique per se. It is based on the assumption stated earlier that behind any patterns of dysfunctional behavior there are valid intentions or needs. At times, especially in working with adolescents or verbally skilled preadolescents, it is useful to "track back" to the intentions or needs. This procedure is demonstrated in the case of Charlie, a stocky, sixteen-year-old with alcoholic parents who were neglectful and generally imposed no limits on and gave no structure to Charlie's life. To add to his problems, Charlie engaged in compulsive stealing—including shoplifting and thefts from neighbors as well as his parents.

Charlie's stealing was somewhat unusual in that he was quite artless about how he stole, and was usually caught and readily admitted to the stealing when confronted. While his probation officer was of the opinion that Charlie was seeking punishment, counselors talking to Charlie eventually came to a different conclusion. It appeared that the only times that Charlie felt attended to by his parents was when he was in trouble. During those times, the parents were obliged to meet with probation officers, go to court, and it was then that they made sporadic efforts at family counseling. The truth, which was more obvious in retrospect, was that Charlie's need for attention was being met in an indirect way through the stealing. Charlie, of course, had been unable to express directly his need for attention from his parents because he anticipated that they could not freely offer it and he would be rebuffed. Understanding this process allowed Charlie and his mother and father to discuss ways for him to request and receive more attention from them.

Most of the common symptoms of abused children—among them aggressiveness, withdrawal, regression, and behavioral acting out—have the quality of being maladaptive "learned" solutions to the child's needs for safety, freedom from fear, self-depreciation, and depression as well as to his needs for attention.

The Therapeutic Catch-22. This is a family of techniques that can at times be useful to move a child from maladaptive to more adaptive responses. The technique is sometimes called "therapeutic paradox." The Therapeutic Catch-22 occurs when the therapist creates a situation for the child in which his maladaptive defenses are redefined to become untenable for the child and, at the same time, the child is encouraged to try new solutions.

In the earlier example involving Max, the therapist used this approach and suggested to the boy that his refusal to talk was a promise that he had made to himself that he should keep. To the extent that the refusal to talk was a control method, designed to frustrate the therapist or other adults, Max was in a situation where both talking and not talking constituted cooperation or "giving in."

His rather creative solution of writing notes solved the dilemma for him and resulted in his participation in the problem-solving—which was more adaptive than his original position of refusing to talk.

It should be noted that use of this type of Catch-22 approach, which is sometimes called "paradoxical intentions," is in some states, such as New York, not approved and can be used only under very special circumstances. In any case, this procedure should be used only by well-trained professionals with great gentleness and care.

Another example of Therapeutic Catch-22 is found in the following exchange between fifteen-year-old Juan and his therapist.

Juan was a slender, handsome boy with dark, impenetrable eyes who had been arrested for shoplifting while on one of his frequent runaways from home. Juan had been passed back and forth between his divorced parents, usually because of severe conflicts with one or the other of his two stepparents. He had most recently lived with his father and stepmother. The stepmother resented Juan's misbehavior, including his aggression and resentment toward her two younger children by a prior marriage. She expressed her resentment through frequent ridicule and demeaning of Juan. In the following segment of his counseling, Juan was describing his conflict with his stepmother:

JUAN: Susan [his stepmother] hates me. She thinks her own kids are so perfect, and if I don't do everything just right she yells at me and lies to Dad about me.

THERAPIST: She thinks that Becky and Troy [the stepsiblings] are perfect.

JUAN: Yeah, and they get away with all kinds of crap.

THERAPIST: What do they do?

JUAN: Like, they get into my room and get into my stuff, and they listen on the phone when I'm trying to talk to my friends.

THERAPIST: What do you do when they do that?

JUAN: I smack them because Susan never believes me, and anyway she just wants to get rid of me. She doesn't want me around.

THERAPIST: So if the kids do something wrong like get into your room, you hit them and then—

JUAN: Then Susan tells Dad, 'See, this kid has been hitting the little kids and he is nothing but trouble. Send him to his mom." And stuff like that.

THERAPIST: So Susan wants to get rid of you?

JUAN: So she can have Dad for herself.

THERAPIST: And you help her out by hitting the little kids, so she has something to tell your dad?

JUAN: Yeah, I guess that's it.

THERAPIST: So you're going to help Susan win, as far as getting you out, by how you handle the problems with the little kids?

Horsies and Duckies. Working with children in therapy is a unique situation. While therapists are at times thought of as either "adult" or "child" specialists, in reality working with children requires multiple specialties depending on the age of the child. Work with preschoolers, early-school-age, latency-age, and adolescent kids varies—requiring different skills and approaches. In general, the younger the child the more that therapy depends on nonverbal communication.

"Adult specialists" at times enjoy harassing their "child specialist" colleagues about "playing with dolls" and other toys. One rather sensitive child therapist, in ordering play-therapy supplies including dolls, wrote on the order form "four assorted humanoid simulation units." The fact is, with very young children (about three to eight) the play medium is the most effective way of communicating. Through their play fantasies children express and explore their dilemmas conflicts, fears, and other emotions. By entering into the fantasies through play, the therapist can convey an understanding of the child and guide him or her through alternative solutions to problems.

Entry into the fantasies requires that the therapist unself-consciously be a child. This includes among other things making engine noises, sitting on the floor, dressing dolls, and effecting different voices for characters in doll or puppet play. It requires playing "horsies and duckies" without condescension, embarrassment, or boredom. It requires the ability to enter into fantasies and play in order to help the child understand his world and resolve his conflicts.

The following is a report of work with a five-year-old girl titled "Conversations with Linda" that reflects the non-verbal aspect of communication with children:

> One of the children who has been teaching me about therapy is a five-year-old girl who doesn't talk. Her parents brought her to the clinic on the recommendation of a physician who felt she might be retarded. Although at this age neurological examinations aren't entirely reliable, the ones she had did not indicate brain damage.
>
> Linda (not her real name, of course) is an attractive little girl with an expressive face and a lot of energy. My first move was to try and establish her capacity to learn. I used simple games, such as having Linda guess under which of the small boxes I had hidden

an M&M candy. It was quickly apparent that Linda (a) was not about to play by my rules, (b) could always get the candy, and (c) was bored by my games. More or less in self-defense, and after several other observations, I concluded that she was not retarded and proceeded to the treatment phase.

I decided that the most direct approach to get Linda talking would be to use a shaping procedure. As a special inducement, I planned to give her small rewards (candy, potato chips, sips of orange soda) when she made any verbal sounds. After that, I would require a word, several words, and so on in speeches and discourses. So far, Linda has stood on her constitutional rights (the Fifth Amendment, so to speak) and not uttered a sound in order to get one of the prizes I offer her. She will, however, accept them if there are no conditions attached, or she will filch them if they are left unguarded.

Linda showed a particular fondness for orange soda and would point to the machine that doles out bottles for a quarter. Deciding that I hadn't showed enough resolve, I determined to sit with her in front of the machine, quarter in hand, until she made a sound. I would then feed the machine, let Linda get the bottle, and in that way teach her that she can rule the world with her vocal cords. She went home one-half hour later, silent and popless. Although disappointed, I believed I had demonstrated my integrity by not giving in. Since then I have had reason to believe that she may well have felt the same way.

At one point I wondered if Linda could understand speech as well as her parents, and I thought she could. Although she followed most directions, I wondered if this was because she was understanding my gestures and the context of the situation, rather than the language itself. To check on this I spent a half-hour giving her unrelated directions with the delivery of a mannequin. Among other things, I found that she could understand the following: "Close the door." "Now come in the room and close the door." "Pick up the nail, Linda." "Linda, please don't pound the nail in my foot." "Come get a drink of pop." In fact, it seemed that Linda understood and could do about anything I asked. I wondered if I asked her please to talk to me . . .

I don't want to give the impression that Linda and I don't communicate, because we do. The following is a conversation that Linda and I had during part of one session. I used words, Linda used looks and gestures—which I interpreted as follows:

ME *(as I walk into the waiting room):* Hi, Linda, how are you today?

LINDA *(making for the playroom):* Never mind the small talk, let's get to where the toys are. *(We enter the playroom after our ritual of getting a bottle of pop.)*

ME: What would you like to do today?

LINDA: *(Unintelligible.)*

ME: Would you like a drink of pop?

LINDA: Not if you're going to hang on to the bottle.

ME: How about if I put it on the table?

LINDA: I'll think about it.

LINDA *(after examining most of the objects in the room):* Open this bottle of nails.

ME *(opening the bottle):* What are you going to do with them?

LINDA: See this nail?

ME: Yes.

LINDA: *(Dumps them on the floor.)*

LINDA *(going to the game box):* What's in here?

ME: Pick up the nails before you open the game box.

LINDA: I don't want to.

ME *(rising to interfere with her opening the box):* I know, but you have to anyway.

LINDA *(coming over to the nails):* Okay, okay, don't get excited. *(Linda picks up the nails, then gets the bottle of pop from the table and takes a long drink.)*

ME: Do you like the pop?

LINDA *(putting the bottle down):* I can live without it.

These are my interpretations of what transpired. Linda may not have seen it this way and may someday tell me so (I suspect, in no uncertain terms). The interaction occurred at a time when I was not actively trying to elicit sounds or speech from her, but had decided to relax and see if I could understand her.

Linda fascinates me. She shows independence, integrity, negativism, humor, anger, contentment, and all human feelings without the use of words. Somehow I feel talking has taken on some significance for her beyond mere communication.

It's not just that she refused to talk or make sounds, but she actually does less verbalizing when some pressure is being placed on her. This is true even of gentle, kindly pressure. She shows a great deal of ambivalence toward me and other people, seeming to be both attracted and fearful at the same time. Is refusing to talk a way of keeping people at a safe distance? Is it overwhelming responsibility? Does Linda feel that if she gave in to the demand for speech there would be other (unreasonable, in her mind) demands made upon her? Would talking be surrendering her identity or integrity? Is it possible that Linda has come to view her refusal to talk as her claim to individuality? Does she resent attempts to encroach on her individuality and express her resentment through negativism? I don't know as yet when Linda's refusal to talk means, but I have great hopes that if I "listen" closely she will tell me.

Luckily for this therapist and others, children are patient in repeating through their own means the essence of their problems and conflicts, until (at least usually) the therapist is able to understand them. Linda, by the way, did eventually talk.

Working with Adolescents. Adolescents can be the most difficult and, at times, the most frustrating age group for therapists. They are struggling with their urges and fears about becoming independent. They have issues of conformity and defiance that they play out with the therapists. This is a period in their lives when issues of identity self-awareness and relationships with their peers are of utmost importance to them. Adolescents are too big to manage and too immature to self-manage.

Like younger children, adolescents have difficulty talking directly about themselves, their feelings and concerns. They frequently have had negative experiences with adults that they transfer to the therapist—which complicates working with them. They see adults as people who punish and try to control them. They are unsure of themselves and fear being criticized or controlled. Frequently, they deal with these problems by being openly defiant or passively resistant and obstructivistic in treatment.

Adolescents can sometimes deal with their problems through second-person media. Harold, a sixteen-year-old, wrote the following at the urging of therapist who was trying to find a way for him to come to grips with his loneliness and isolation. It was titled "The Deserted Beach."

No one comes to this beach anymore. That is why I like to come here. The gulls come here once in a while, but not very often because there aren't any [people] here to feed them. They fly out over the ebbing tide. Where they go no one knows.

There are miles of long shady beach beaten down hard with surf and sun. It reminds me of an endless desert when the tide is out.

Barren of life, oh so barren, is the beach with its winds coming and going.

As the white clouds flutter by in the morning warmth, the beach looks like a gaunt spectator. No trees for birds to gather. Only the gulls, and they are a passing lot.

When night weaves her web of darkness, the beach seems white and transparent, like it didn't exist. I know it is nothing more than sand. But, alas, this sand has meaning. It is gifted with the virtue of humiliation—this, is as no other is.

In working with adolescents, issues of trust and confidentiality become very important. Troubled youth, especially those adolescents who have been abused, are distrustful of adults and frequently expect some collusion between the therapist (an adult) and their parents (more adults). It is generally helpful to clearly establish and communicate rules of confidentiality, informing the adolescents that the content of what they talk about will not be shared with others, including parents, except under three conditions: (1) if the young person divulges information that puts him/her at risk, such as suicide, planning runaways, criminal acts, etc.; (2) if he/she divulges some further abuse that the law requires be reported; and (3) if he/she gives permission to pass along to parents, teachers, caseworkers, etc., information that will be helpful in the treatment process. On the other side of the coin is the parents' need to know about and be involved in the treatment process of their child. Normally, adolescents are willing to give permission to provide general information to their parents, but their sense of control of this is important.

When using a family therapy approach, confidentiality issues are less acute, since the parents are present. Where there has been severe abuse, however, the adolescent frequently needs the freedom and support that is more available through the individual approach.

When working with abused adolescents, it is important to offer support and encouragement without fixing the child in the role of victim. That is, while being aware of the tremendous damage that is done to adolescents through the abuse they have experienced, it is important to recognize that the response pattern they have developed to cope with the abuse often is maladaptive in dealing with people in general. The approach of undermining maladaptive emotional, cognitive, and behavioral responses and providing experience with constructive alternatives has been described before, and is represented in the exchange between Charlene and her counselor.

Suzanne, age fourteen, was taller and, although not obese, was heavier than her age mates. Her mother had left the family for parts unknown when she was three and her father subsequently married a woman with two younger boys when Suzanne was six. While well-meaning, Suzanne's stepmother (and later, adoptive mother) was very conscious of appearance, style, and weight. She initially doted on Suzanne, but as Suzanne entered puberty at about age twelve and began to be tall and put on weight, the adoptive mother became increasingly critical, demanding, and rejecting. By all accounts, she also clearly favored her own sons, who were four and three years younger than Suzanne. When Suzanne rebelled against the rejection and what she perceived to be preferential treatment of her stepbrothers, her mother responded with exacerbating harshness that led to sadistic abuse, including beatings with a belt.

The following excerpt was during the third counseling session, while Suzanne was in a temporary foster home following a runaway. Suzanne, in the first two sessions, had been sullen and withdrawn, answering questions, when she did at all, with mumbled single-word replies.

THERAPIST: Hello, Suzanne. Nice to see you again.

SUZANNE (*rolling her eyes skyward*): Yeah, sure.

THERAPIST: Have you thought about any of the things we discussed last time?

SUZANNE: (*Shakes her head and looks at her hands.*)

THERAPIST: You haven't had time or it's not important to you or . . .

SUZANNE: It's stupid.

THERAPIST: What part was stupid?

SUZANNE: The whole thing is stupid.

THERAPIST: It's you and your life we are talking about. I don't think that's stupid.

SUZANNE: That's because *you're* stupid.

THERAPIST: Are you saying that if I was smart and wasn't stupid, I wouldn't waste time with you?

SUZANNE: I guess so. Yeah.

THERAPIST: Well, I haven't felt like it is a waste of time. I've wanted to see you.

SUZANNE: Yeah, sure. You're only here because you have to be.

THERAPIST: How do you know that?

SUZANNE: *(No response.)*

THERAPIST: Is everyone stupid who wants to spend time with you—or just me?

SUZANNE: Everyone. . . . No one wants to spend time with me.

THERAPIST: You work very hard at discouraging people from spending time with you or being with you. Does it usually work?

SUZANNE: What do you mean?

THERAPIST: Are you usually able to get people to stay away from you.

SUZANNE: I don't want people to stay away from me, but they want to on their own.

THERAPIST: Telling them they are stupid, not looking at them, and acting bored will probably discourage most people.

SUZANNE: They don't like me because I'm fat and ugly and I can't do anything right.

THERAPIST: Wrong, kiddo. They avoid you because you believe all that nonsense about yourself and because you treat them badly.

SUZANNE: But look at how I've been treated—

THERAPIST: I know, and that's a good reason to stay away from people who treated you bad, but it isn't a good reason to treat other people bad.

SUZANNE: That's easy for you to say, but you don't know what it is like to be me.

THERAPIST: You're right. I don't know, but I would like to.

In this brief exchange, the therapist redefined some key elements of Suzanne's way of looking at herself and others. Without attacking Suzanne, she focused Suzanne on her behavior and how it affected others, and she conveyed recognition and understanding of the girl's pain. When Suzanne referred to her belief that people "don't like me," the therapist redefined that as "They avoid you." Most important, Suzanne's negative, unresponsive behavior did not drive the therapist away from her. As stated earlier, a child's experience with a therapist needs to be: "My defenses aren't working, but I'm safe anyway."

10

Therapy with Parents

Treatment of abusing parents has much in common with approaches to therapy with adults in general. As with children, there is a range of treatment, variously emphasizing the cognitive, emotional, or behavioral components of the person. Abusing parents may have mental or emotional problems that require treatment apart from any concern about the parent role or function. Abusing parents may be thought disordered (at times they are described as being psychotic or mentally ill); they may have substance-abuse problems (drugs and/or alcohol); and they may, and frequently do, have situational problems, personality and anxiety disorders, as well as other problems.

In addition to focusing on whatever mental health problems the parent may have, there are some common problems represented by abusing parents that are of concern primarily because they impact their behavior toward their children. These include, as cited earlier, poor self-esteem, social isolation, poor interpersonal skills, ignorance about child care and management, life stresses, problems with anger and resentment, and a lack of the ability to be assertive. Before discussing these particular problems, it should be noted that abusing parents frequently come to a counselor or a therapy program or facility under circumstances and with attitudes that are countertherapeutic.

It is common for abusing parents to come to treatment, under protest, at the direction of a court or under pres-

sure from caseworkers. Sometimes there have been pre-
liminary court hearings about allegations of abuse
wherein the parents have been found "guilty of abuse
and/or neglect" and are "sentenced to treatment." This
adversary, coercive, accusatory context is diametrically opposed to the usual treatment process, in which the client
comes voluntarily for help, with self-defined problems
and concerns and with a sense of shared goals and trust
of the therapist. Furthermore, the trust and confidentiality
issues are compromised by the fact that frequently a counselor or therapist will be obligated by law, or compelled
by court order, to report to the court and/or child protective agencies the parents' progress or lack of progress and
any disclosures that bear on the well-being of the child
or children involved. At times, these problems are exacer-
bated by zealous defense attorneys who have an obligation
to protect their clients' self-interest regardless of the consequences to the child or the therapeutic process. The
bizarre spectacle of a client invoking the Fifth Amendment in counseling sessions has often been a reality. Counselors and therapists have wondered if they are not
required to read incoming clients their "Miranda rights."

While such problems are handicapping to the treatment
process, they are not fatal. The situation requires, however, that the respective obligations and responsibilities
of both professional and parent be clear and mutually
understood. Ultimately, the parent client has to understand that progress in treatment depends on the parent's
participating fully in the treatment process. This participation will be encouraged and enhanced to the extent
that the stated treatment goals make sense to him or her
and are goals that, once achieved, will be of intrinsic value
to the parent; i.e., be self-perpetuating.

Treatment goals should be explicit, specific, credible,
and functional. Expectations (usually through written
statements of goals) help the therapist and parent focus
on the work to be accomplished and reduce the chances

for misunderstanding. Specific goals are usually those that describe goal behavior, about which there would be agreement between client and therapist as to whether and when they are achieved. Generally, specific goals describe target behaviors. "Being a better parent" is general and not grounded in observations that can readily be shared by client and therapist. "Getting compliance from the child through nonphysical methods" is better. The credibility of a goal refers to whether or not the client can identify with it and see its relevance. Goal statements such as "improve super-ego controls" or "get in touch with feelings" may be understood and relevant to the therapist but will generally not be credible to parent clients. Goals such as "Do not discipline while angry" and "Express hurt rather than anger when you're feeling hurt" would be more credible.

Functional goals are goals that, when achieved, become self-reinforcing or self-perpetuating. They are goals that will begin to offer intrinsic rewards to the parent.

Jerry, a mountain of a man, had been abusive to his wife, a diminutive but verbally quick and sharp-tongued person, and went through domestic violence counseling. He learned some self-control methods that prevented him from lashing out at his wife, but he stored the anger and began venting it on his two teenage children. While in counseling for his abusive behavior toward the children, the problem of displacement of anger from his wife onto his children became the focus. Jerry was a man of "few words," who had never learned to represent himself verbally, relying instead on his fists. He was taught to engage his wife verbally and confront her criticisms by verbal means, through the "fair fighting" techniques espoused by George Bach. This developing skill of handling verbal confrontations allowed him to deal with his wife as well as with his own anger, and the success was rewarding to Jerry, becoming a part of his normal behavior.

While it is generally true that abusing parents use ineffectual, misguided, and destructive approaches to discipline and managing their children, there are, with few exceptions, worthy, legitimate needs, intentions and goals behind the parent's dysfunctional behavior. These are usually confused or are fused in the parent's mind so that he or she sees these responses as a necessary and inevitable consequence of his or her needs or intentions and the children's behavior. Criticism or condemnation of parents' abusive behavior is perceived as criticism of themselves. It is essential that parents' legitimate needs and intentions be both validated and separated from nonfunctional parental behaviors. This is usually more successfully accomplished by starting with a validation of the needs, intentions, etc., and then finding more effective ways of meeting the needs or intentions. Behind the abusive behavior is usually some aspect of wanting to get the child to comply, be socialized, keep the child from harm, be respected, be a good parent, and be loved.

Joe and Melody were referred for treatment after their ten-year-old son, Jason, had complained to his teacher about harsh treatment by his father. Specifically, the father was grounding Jason for several weeks at a time for being late in getting home from school, not completing his chores, and sassing his mother. When Jason violated the restrictions (no television, no playing with the computer, staying in his room except for meals and bathroom breaks), his father resorted to whippings with a belt. The day Jason complained to his teacher, he had physical welts on his leg, back, and buttocks.

The family situation was complicated. Joe was a domineering and angry man, having been raised by strict, punitive parents and being a "self-made" man who made his own way in life from age fourteen. Melody was very passive and compliant. She attempted to buffer Jason and his younger brother against her husband's harshness, and at times she entered into collusion with the boys to hide infractions or problems from their father. She disagreed with her husband's harshness but did not feel she could deal with it directly, allowing her sons (especially Jason) to vent their anger on her through back talk, disobedience, and even open disparagement of her.

In a court hearing the boys were made dependents of the court but allowed to remain in the home on the condition that the family be put in counseling. Joe's attitude on coming into counseling was that the state was interfering in his family life: Jason was an incorrigible child who required a firm hand, and his wife was partly to blame for not backing him more fully in his discipline. His words to the counselor were, "I am here because I have to be. . . . I'll listen, but there isn't any need for this."

In talking to Joe, it became clear that: (a) he interpreted his son's disobedience as an attack on his parental authority, (b) he felt impotent and isolated in the family, and, (c) he knew little about appropriate limits. In an abortive previous counseling attempt, he had quit when the counselor identified the treatment goals as "to improve Joe's parenting." Joe interpreted the goal as blaming *him* for the problem. He felt more comfortable with the goal "Find ways to get Jason to comply with reasonable rules."

Treatment was subsequently focused on defining "reasonable rules" and convincing Joe of the greater effectiveness of natural consequences for infractions and the principles of effective use of punishment; i.e., immediacy and moderation. Defining the problem of his response to Jason's misbehavior as a matter of effectiveness, rather than in terms of right or wrong, allowed Joe to change how he responded to the boy without requiring that he identify himself as being bad or wrong. When Jason responded with improved behavior, the new approaches were validated, as was Joe in his parent role. Other issues—including Jason's resentment and the necessity of Melody's sharing the burden of discipline—were also handled.

All people come into treatment with a unique set of

attitudes, styles, and problems; and the treatment approach must also be unique. There are, however, some generalizations that can be applied to broad categories of problems. It is necessary to emphasize that not all parents can be treated or will cooperate with treatment to the extent needed for the safety of their children, and there are times when the well-being of children dictates removal of them from the parents permanently.

The Mentally Ill Parent. This represents a special problem in that the mental illness may be unmanageable to the point where the child's safety and well-being are at serious risk. Despite those rare situations in which mentally ill parents seriously harm or kill the child, the most common consequence to a child of having a mentally ill parent is neglect. Children of mentally ill parents often do not receive the necessary basic caretaking: hygiene, health care, food, shelter, etc. They are at times subjected to the parent's bizarre views of the world and may become enmeshed in a psychotic parent's delusional system. Depending on the age of the child when the parent's psychotic symptoms appear, the availability of other support systems, and the effectiveness of treatment for the parent, the child may be too endangered by the parent's illness to allow him or her to remain in the home. In general, the younger the child, the more serious the parent's symptoms; and the fewer the support systems available, the higher the risk to the child.

Any treatment for the abusing or neglecting mentally ill parent must focus initially on the illness itself. Illnesses such as schizophrenia and affective disorders (depression, bipolar disorder, etc.) can often be successfully treated with a combination of medication and psychotherapy. The parent must have available appropriate psychiatric treatment and must cooperate with the treatment in order for there to be a chance for successfully maintaining the parent/child relationship.

110 | Child Abuse

Jane, a slender mother, experienced what was diagnosed as a delusional disorder. While ordinarily not bizarre in her behavior, she was concerned that her children, Karen, age eleven, and Abe, age eight, would be at risk for assault, kidnapping, or drug use if they attended public schools. She further believed that being outdoors was dangerous in that the children would get cancer because of the depletion of the ozone layer.

Jane frequently kept the children from school because of her fears and sent them only under duress. She exaggerated or fabricated symptoms of illness in the children as a reason to keep them home. She avoided intervention for years by moving frequently from school district to school district. When the courts finally intervened, the children were far behind in school, poorly socialized, and had begun to share the mother's paranoid thinking, being fearful of strangers (anyone except the immediate family) and having excessive unrealistic health concerns. Jane was resistant to treatment, seeing therapeutic efforts as both unnecessary and as attempts to carry out plots of "mind control." She eventually refused treatment and the children were permanently removed from her care.

Personality Disorders. These are probably the most common diagnoses given to abusing parents. The general category of personality disorder includes such specific disorders as antisocial, narcissistic, borderline, histrionic, avoidant, dependent, obsessive-compulsive, passive-aggressive, paranoid, schizoid, and schizotypal. The name of each of these subcategories generally identifies the most important type of symptom of each disorder. The most common personality disorders among abusing parents are the *antisocial, borderline, narcissistic,* and *passive-aggressive* subtypes.

Antisocial disorders are characterized by antisocial attitudes and behavior, including a disrespect for laws and social norms of behavior, impulsivity, shallow interpersonal relationships, and anger or resentment. People with this disorder frequently violate laws and frequently have criminal histories. Their abuse of their children derives from their poorly controlled anger, indifference to the welfare of others (including their children), a rather single-minded seeking of self-gratification, and the poor modeling these parents provide for their children. This disorder is extremely difficult to treat because of the symptoms listed above. Often, parental rights are terminated, usually after a long period struggling to help them change. Tragically, this is usually after severe psychological damage to the children has occurred.

Where it is undertaken, treatment for parents with antisocial personality disorders focuses on training in responsibility, accountability, anger management, and impulse control. Therapy requires the development of an alliance and relationship between the therapist and the patient or client, and motivation on the part of the client to make changes. Since people with the antisocial disorder have great difficulty with trust and in forming relationships, and since motivation is typically poor, treatment for these people is frequently unsuccessful. A chance of treating people with this disorder usually requires external pressure, courts, probation officers, and frequently out-of-home placement of the child.

One creative psychiatrist who managed a hospital unit consisting largely of antisocial patients used an anxiety-induction procedure to create a motivation for treatment called the "wheel of fortune." This consisted of a carnival-type wheel that had a variety of activities posted around the perimeter ranging from very positive ("Go to town and see a movie") to very negative ("Scrub all of the urinals and toilets"). Patients who were placed on the wheel spun it each morning to learn what their day's activities would be. Since the people who are antisocial depend greatly on their manipulative skills to manage other people, and since there was no way to manage "the wheel," it produced anxiety and these patients would usually work in therapy to get themselves removed from the procedure. While it seemed effective at the time (many years ago), very likely the technique would not past muster today with civil liberties attorneys.

Patients with borderline personality disorders are only slightly, if at all, less difficult to treat than those with the antisocial disorder. These parents are very emotionally labile, have frequent transient and destructive mate-relationships, are immature, and are subject to temper outbursts, bouts of depression, and suicide attempts. Impulsively, they hurt and neglect their children and subject them to chaotic and unstable lives as they go through their own serial destructive relationships. They also provide children with poor modeling of family life and interpersonal behavior. They are, in fact, quite similar to people with the antisocial personality disorder, and professionals often dispute which category fits a particular person. Treatment for borderline personalities consists of a focus on establishing and maintaining interpersonal boundaries, developing impulse controls, distinguishing reality from fantasy, and developing the ability to maintain appropriate emotional or relationship ties.

Narcissistic-personality disordered parents tend to lack empathy with others and are grandiose and unrealistic about themselves. They are manipulative and require rather constant adulation and approval from others. This pattern of symptoms results—for the children—in emotional and physical neglect, a lack of empathy and emotional support, and intense and at times chaotic emotional experiences. Neglect is more common than abuse in a family with narcissistic parents, and again it is a difficult disorder to treat—although not as difficult as the antisocial and borderline disorders.

Treatment for narcissistic parents is most effectively geared toward repairing the poor self-esteem and self-doubt that underlie the narcissism. Often these people were raised in a home where they were indulged but not supported. Their families frequently included parents who, themselves, were narcissistic and too preoccupied with their own needs and interests to attend to those of their children. This experience with emotional indifference and indulgence set the stage for developing a pattern of self-absorption and self-love (narcissism). The self-love was a replacement for the reassurance of being loved and respected by others. Therapy is directed toward changing attitudes and behavior patterns to break this narcissistic trap and allow the person to receive and give reassurance and affection in his or her interactions with others, including the children.

The passive-aggressive disorder may be among the easiest of the personality disorders to treat. People with this disorder basically are passive people who use the displacement and avoidance mechanisms. They express unresolved resentment or anger through procrastination, manipulation, obstructionism, and covert criticism and blaming. Occasionally they act out their anger and aggression against their children. The risk to children is that they are a relatively safe target for the parent's displaced resentment or anger. Sporadic, stress-triggered physical abuse is the most common form of abuse. These parents usually have the capacity to feel regret and some motivation to change this pattern.

Treatment for the passive-aggressive-disordered parent focuses on developing appropriate assertiveness and self-esteem. To the extent that the person can come to confront stresses, conflicts, and problems in a direct manner, he or she improves in both self-esteem and self-confidence and loses the need to displace anger onto others in order to manipulate and to avoid the problem. Passive-aggressive people often have a history of troubled relationships with parents, or other caregivers, who were usually critical and demanding and at times threatening. Dealing with some of these relationship issues—especially where the passive-aggressive parent has the opportunity to redefine the relationships with his or her own parents—can also be helpful.

One of the types of child abuse that appears to be relatively rare and usually involves some kind of underlying personality disorder is Munchausen's Syndrome by proxy.

Munchausen's Syndrome by proxy (MSBP) has potentially very serious consequences to children. This disorder involves symptoms of anxiety as well as personality problems, and consists of the parents' seeking or insisting on intrusive and frequently dangerous medical care for their child. Such parents will fake medical symptoms in the child in order to get medical intervention, and they have been known to starve or poison their children in these efforts. Not only are actions such as poisoning or starving children dangerous, but the child is put at serious risk through unnecessary follow-up medical treatment, such as operations and medical tests at the parents' insistence. Parents' reporting inaccurate or fake symptoms to doctors—who have to depend on parental information in their treatment and diagnosis—means further risk to the child. These parents are often bright and medically sophisticated, and they tend to "doctor shop" until they find a compliant physician or they change doctors when one becomes resistant to their requests for treatment of their child.

Lilly, a parent who was eventually diagnosed with MSBP, took her two-year-old son, Donny, to a doctor stating that the child had blood in his diaper and that while she was changing his diaper, he had urinated blood. The pediatrician was puzzled since he could find nothing in the initial examination that would account for the symptoms described by Lilly. The soiled diaper had been discarded and was not available for examination.

To be safe, the doctor admitted the child to the hospital for observation and ordered urine samples to be taken.

The samples found that there was, in fact, blood in the urine. On further checking, however, it was found that the blood type was not that of the child but was the same as that of the mother. While Lilly denied having anything to do with contaminating the urine sample, the doctor appropriately made a referral to the child protective service agency. Because of concern about the potential seriousness of the risk to the child if the mother did fit the syndrome, the child was removed from the home and a psychological evaluation was ordered.

In the psychological evaluation that involved both the mother and the father, there was not a great amount of pathology noted. The parents had grown up in a Southern state and had been in the present area for about a year. There had been significant family estrangement in the case of Lilly. Her husband had, at one time, been in the armed services, but left at Lilly's insistence because of the long periods of time that she was alone while he was overseas. The father was unemployed and had had difficulty in finding employment, even though he was trained in a technical field. He was supportive of his wife, believing that she was a good mother and that she was not in any way responsible for the laboratory findings. Neither parent was found to be thought-disordered. Both were of average intelligence, although Lilly in particular was somewhat poorly educated. Lilly was quite gregarious, her husband more quiet and reserved. There were some marital conflicts and problems in communication and Lilly was found to be rather insecure and dependent. It was noted that there was some anxiety and stress based on the family being isolated from the extended family, the lack of employment, and financial problems as well as the current problems with the child protective service.

Psychological testing, including MMPIs (a widely used personality test), did not indicate severe pathology, although personality problems were present. MSBP is diagnosed by case history, and since there was no resolution between Lilly's version of the child's health problems and the laboratory findings, the couple was told that Lilly probably had the disorder. A report was made back to the court, and it resulted in a continuation of the placement of the child outside the home.

Subsequent to the evaluation, the evaluator was asked to provide therapy for the couple. The treatment initially consisted of therapy appointments twice a week, including a combination of individual therapy with Lilly and couples' treatment. In the course of the first phase of treatment, which was fairly intensive, the mother revealed additional information about her history. Part of this was that she, herself, had a long-term chronic, undiagnosed condition involving her kidneys. She reported that she would periodically have blood in her urine and that as a child she had numerous hospitalizations and medical procedures, including some operations. Lilly also reported that she had been the victim of serious sexual abuse at the hands of her father when she was an adolescent. Apparently this was not reported to authorities and was handled essentially by the family themselves. She had one brief marriage in her late teens, which did not result in children. She also reported having had numerous miscarriages, as well as having been hospitalized at about age twenty, when she was obviously suicidal.

In individual work with Lilly, she was initially steadfast in her denial of any participation in contaminating the child's urine samples or in fabricating any of the child's symptoms. She did express a lot of concern about her own health problems, as well as those of the child, and was of course upset about being separated from her child. In the course of talking with Lilly about her childhood experiences, including the sexual assaults, it was clear that she had not fully come to terms with these and had many of the characteristics of victims of sexual assault: self-blame, self-depreciation, fear of the person who had assaulted her (her father), feelings of unworthiness, and distorted attitudes about sexuality.

In talking abut her prior psychiatric hospitalization, Lilly indicated that the precipitating event occurred when she found herself in a vehicle, "spaced out," with her child in the car. She felt that she may have been suicidal and may have represented a risk to her infant at that time. She talked about other times when she "spaced out." The therapist decided to approach Lilly by suggesting to her that it was possible she contaminated the urine sample in the hospital during a period when she was in such a condition and that if this were the case, she would gradually come to remember this through dreams or other similar cognitive experiences.

Over the next few weeks, Lilly reported having dreams that she had contaminated the sample. They eventually progressed to the point where she said that she had an active memory of having done so. Initially, she could not remember how she accomplished the contamination, but eventually she reported that she remembered having bitten the inside of her mouth, spitting the blood into the urine sample. At the point where Lilly first admitted to contaminating the urine sample, a joint meeting was held with her husband and her husband's father and step-mother, who had moved into the area and were providing some emotional and financial support for the family. Lilly made a confession and discussed with her husband the actions she had taken, seeking forgiveness, etc. Her husband was reasonably understanding and supportive.

The next series of appointments was focused on helping Lilly understand the motive, or basis, for her behavior. The most reasonable explanation seemed to be that the MSBP behavior was designed to obtain attention from her husband and other people, and to "tie" or "bind" her husband closer to her. In the course of talking to her, it was discovered that the "bloody diaper" episode occurred during a time that her husband was out of town (against her wishes), looking for employment. It was also discovered that Lilly was quite jealous and was fearful of other women taking her husband away from her. During the course of treatment, Lilly engaged in some behavior that replicated the MSBP dynamics, albeit in a less pathological way. For example, she made a false report that "two black men" had attempted to break into her home. This occurred when her husband was out of town.

Additional treatment time was devoted to remedial work (along with crisis management), including helping Lilly to improve her self-concept and the ability to communicate her needs and wishes in a more effective way. She was coached in making clear, direct requests of her husband, the purpose being to give her healthy alternative ways of meeting her needs. There was also work with the couple in terms of their communication. It was found that they communicated poorly, particularly around areas of differences or intense feelings. Both were cooperative in making some changes in their mode of communication.

At about six months into treatment, the husband was able to locate employment in a city approximately 100 miles distant. There was a period of time when the husband moved to this new city to establish a home and start his work and before Lilly was able to join him.

Health concerns were a cause for major upheavals and anxiety on the part of all concerned. While her son on a second trial placement in the home, Lilly discovered that he had head lice, and while she generally handled it appropriately, her shaving her son's head was seen by the state caseworker as symptomatic of the syndrome and as evidence of lack of progress. Lilly at times became concerned about her son's diet, which again was cause for concern. Despite these problems and others related to tensions between the caseworker, who was very anxious about the child's well-being, and the therapist, who was more positive about Lilly's rehabilitation prospects, the child was eventually returned. On six-month follow up, the family was reunited and doing well.

Work on the foregoing case was complicated and made dificult by a variety of factors, most of them inherent in working with child abuse in general or with the MSBP syndrome in particular. One of these complications was the basic dilemma found by therapists and abusing parents with any kind of abuse situation. This involves the adversary nature of the legal system, which is imposed into the consulting room. The legal intervention is based on the strength of proof of abuse. On the other hand, treatment is predicated on admission of the abuse by the parents. There is natural concern, not totally unfounded, that such admissions, while therapeutically necessary, may result in harsher or more intrusive actions by the legal system.

The politico-social climate of the state was also a factor. There had recently been a child death (due to physical abuse) for which the state social agency had been publicly criticized. State workers were nervous about taking chances with the welfare of Lilly's child because of the freshness of the tragedy, and were understandably inclined to "play it safe." The adversary atmosphere of the legal system was further brought into the treatment in that people involved in the case tended to line up on the side of the prosecution or the defense, depending on their roles. This resulted in some very difficult and heated staffings around the case. It also meant that working with it became very time-consuming in order to keep information from becoming distorted as it passed through the various channels to the "players."

At the conclusion of treatment, the therapist was not certain whether Lilly's initial denial of the MSBP behavior was a conscious denial to avoid the consequences of her behavior or an unconscious process. She was, however, given an avenue for remembering or admitting that ena-

bled her to salvage her self-worth and move to the remedial phase of treatment.

It is clear that the critical turning point in this case
was the willingness on the part of Lilly to accept responsibility for and admit to the MSBP behavior, including the
exact manner in which she contaminated the laboratory
sample for her son. She was terrified that making such
an admission would result in her being rejected by her
husband, her family, and the therapist as well as permanent termination of her parental rights. The therapist's
position with her was that while that he could not guarantee she would not be rejected by her husband and family,
or that her parental rights would not be terminated, he
would guarantee that if she did not come to terms with
the behavior and admit to the problem, it was most likely
that she *would* eventually lose her parental rights—either
through being seen as a treatment failure or through her
repetition of the MSBP behavior.

Lilly's admission and willingness to deal with her behavior permitted the treatment to focus on remediation and
finding solutions for the underlying psychological problems. In this particular case, the dynamics of the abuse
were that Lilly used a fake illness of her child to gain
attention and to control her husband and bind him to
her. This coping style came out of her own history of
abuse and personal insecurity, including a fear of medical
problems and a fear of losing her husband. It was aided
and abetted by the poor communication between husband
and wife and their inability to deal with their differences
and conflicts. The problem was in part due to Lilly's lack
of skill in making direct requests to meet her needs, as
well as her lack of confidence in her ability to solve problems and receive nurturing, attention, or caretaking just
because of who she was. It was a combination of ignorance, fear, and insecurity that shaped her behavior.
These elements were ultimately the things requiring remediation.

Substance-abusing Parents Who Abuse Their Children.
This represents another difficult treatment problem. Parents who abuse alcohol or drugs, or some combination of both, are high risk for all types of abuse and neglect. Alcohol, as well as most drugs, has the effect of impairing the person's judgment, and it can be disinhibiting. Parents will neglect or physically or sexually abuse their children while under the influence of chemicals, whereas they would not do so otherwise. Drugs and alcohol are addictive either in a psychological or chemical sense. Apart from resulting in specific abusive or neglectful behaviors, such chemical dependencies have a high probability of causing marital and relationship problems, criminal behavior, and financial stress, all of which by themselves contribute to the risk of abusive behavior.

Most (though not all) people who are drug- or alcohol-dependent have one of the personality disorders discussed earlier. These complicate treatment of these people. General wisdom is that the substance abuse must be treated before the personality disorder or other mental problem—and before the specific problem, malparenting or abuse—can be successfully treated. At the very least, the substance-abusing parent must be drug free and in concurrent substance-abuse treatment for there to be a chance of successful management of the abuse and neglect problem.

Cherry was an attractive woman with an infectious laugh and a direct, penetrating manner. She was also a heroin addict who had, in addition, extensively used marijuana, cocaine, and alcohol. She had a history of prostitution, which was in part to support her drug habit and was also, at least initially, a form of revenge against a philandering husband. Her three children were removed from her care because of her substance-abuse problem and she was faced with termination of her parental rights. In response to this threat, she underwent a detoxification (drug withdrawal) program under a physician's care and entered both psychological and drug counseling. Random urinalyses showed her to be free from illicit drugs for a three-month period. Eventually she was taken off the drugs prescribed by her physician, obtained a psychological evaluation, and was quite optimistic about her prospects for rehabilitation. Things were looking up for Cherry, but five weeks later she was found dead from an accidental overdose of heroin.

Cherry's case is far too common, if not in terms of her death by overdose, at least in terms of her returning to drug abuse after a period of progress and then a period of being drug-free. Substance-abusing parents are among the most difficult to treat, and when the addiction is long-term and severe, special care must be taken to protect the children.

11

Special Problems

The first problem in the whole arena of child abuse is a problem of definition. While we all assume we know child abuse when we see it, it is more difficult to define child abuse or neglect in a way that satisfies all of the variety of attitudes regarding parenting, cultural differences, intentions on the part of the parent, and effects on children. Since mandated intervention in abuse situations, and the resulting interference in the parent/child relationship (itself a sacred, protected relationship), are rooted in legal statutes, definitions of what does and does not constitute abuse and neglect are crucial. All fifty states have child abuse statutes and definitions. They vary widely in terms of content and elaboration. One of the least precise definitions was included in the Child Abuse Prevention and Treatment Act of 1974 (PL93–247, 93rd Congress, Senate 1191, 1974). It states in part:

> physical or mental injury, sexual abuse, negligent treatment or maltreatment of a child under the age of 18 by a person who is responsible for the child's welfare under circumstances which indicate the child's health and welfare is harmed or threatened thereby.

The key words *injury, abuse, neglect, maltreatment, harmed,* and *threatened* still require further definition.

While people working with and concerned about child

124 | Child Abuse

abuse and neglect will necessarily be limited by the state statutes where they live, there are some common underpinnings. These include: (a) that the person doing the abusing has some caretaking responsibility (otherwise a physical assault is covered under criminal statutes), (b) that the injury or harm was inflicted in a nonaccidental manner or with disregard for the safety or well-being of the child, and (c) that the harmful act resulted in actual harm or the risk of bodily, intellectual, or emotional harm to the child. This last provision includes specific acts committed, as well as failure to act; for example, failure to provide food, safety, education, medical treatment, etc.

All fifty states have reporting laws regarding child abuse. That is, all states have statutes defining who *may*, without fear of legal reprisal, report suspected instances of child abuse and neglect and who *must* report, under threat of civil or criminal penalty. Generally speaking, anyone is permitted to report to law enforcement or child protective agencies any suspected instances of abuse or neglect. Usually this can be done anonymously, and invariably without putting the person in a position of being liable. While this has resulted in instances of false reports that harass, it permits intervention that otherwise may not have been possible. The nuisance of false, inaccurate reports is a price worth paying for the protection of children.

There are, in addition, a number of persons who are *mandated* to report, under threat of prosecution. While the lists of such mandated people vary from state to state, they generally include physicians, mental health professionals of all types, nurses and other health care professionals, teachers, coroners, day care workers, law enforcement personnel, and administrators of schools, hospitals, and child care facilities. Some states also require reporting by religious healers, ministers, parents, and, in a few cases, attorneys.

Making Reports. Generally, reports are to be made to law enforcement officials or child protective officials. The latter are typically a part of a state agency called, variously, Department of Social and Health Services, Department of Human Services, Department of Health and Welfare, etc. Usually, reporting should be done to law enforcement if the child is in immediate risk or danger, and to the child protection agency otherwise. Most phone books have an emergency number for child protective services on the inside front cover, or at a minimum there is usually a 911 or other emergency number to call in the event of an immediate risk or danger to a child. The operative word in mandated reporting of child abuse is "suspected." That is, the reporting person is neither required to be sure of abuse or neglect nor to prove it. Proof is the job of the investigating agencies, either law enforcement or child protective services.

The problem with reporting is somewhat more difficult when the concerned person has some kind of ongoing relationship with the suspected abuser. For example, information about possible abuse sometimes comes to light in the course of psychological or medical treatment for other types of problems. Reporting, in such cases, runs the risk of destroying or impairing an important working relationship. It has generally been helpful to discuss the problem in a forthright manner with the apparent abusing person in order to let him or her have the option of reporting voluntarily to the appropriate agency. Doing so gives the person more feeling of being in control and puts him or her in a cooperative stance with the investigative agency. Such a scenario should always be accompanied by a follow-up call to ensure that the reporting was done. But whether or not reporting jeopardizes a relationship, causes the loss of a friendship, or creates animosity, it must be done. The potential consequences to the child require it.

The Legal System. The legal system is at the same time a help and a hindrance in work with child abuse. State laws and statutes provide the authority, as well as the obligation, to intervene in situations in which children are being abused. Abusing parents often do not see their actions as detrimental to the child, either because the behavior follows norms and patterns they experienced as children or because the parents are defensive about the accusation that they are being abusive. While some parents are concerned about their own behavior and seek help without being pressured to do so, or cooperate fully with child protective and law enforcement intervention, they are in the minority, and so the laws are necessary for the protection of the majority of abused children who are identified.

The legal system, however, is a mixed blessing. While it provides for intervention where parents are resistant to change or help, the system by its nature complicates work with such families, especially after the initial investigation. Child abuse is a cycle or reciprocating set of behaviors and attitudes on the part of child and parent. The problem can best be dealt with by changing the cycle rather than "breaking it." Breaking the cycle too often represents fracturing the parent-child relationship. A fault line between parent and child is created when there is an investigation of abuse. It is common in investigations—especially when the abuse is serious—for the child to be removed from the parents, at least for a short time. This is done both to prevent the child from being exposed to the parent's anger about the investigation and to protect the child from further abuse or to prevent the parent from pressuring the child to recant statements about abusive parental behavior.

The adversary nature of the legal system has a tendency to exacerbate this parent-child fault line. As mentioned earlier, regardless of the exact language, parents will experience being found guilty of abuse ("abuse substantiated") and being sentenced to treatment. The language referring to compulsory treatment is couched in terms of a "service plan," or other similar language, in a court or dispositional order. In the process itself, the parties are represented by attorneys.

For the parents there are public defenders or private attorneys (where the parents have sufficient financial resources), and representing the state (caseworker) is a district attorney, attorney general, or prosecuting attorney. At times there is also a guardian *ad litem* to represent the child or children; the guardian is usually also an attorney but may be a lay person. Legal ethics demand that the attorneys involved represent their clients' interests to the best of their abilities, so the format is adversary, each side seeking to prove or demonstrate the validity of its client's position. At times all or some of the attorneys are able to work together for what they can define as a common interest in protecting the child and preserving the parent-child relationship, but too often this overall goal is lost in the battle to win the case. This is especially true of the public defender or other attorney representing the parent or parents, who operates in a way similar to his or her way with criminal cases: His or her job, as defined by professional ethics, is to "get the client off," regardless of the "guilt" or "innocence" issues.

The legal position is that out of the adversary scenario the truth, by and large, will emerge and justice will be done. However well this works in criminal proceedings, it is generally destructive in domestic situations such as abuse and neglect. The process almost inevitably results in estrangement between the parents and child, parents and state representative, and usually embroils in the conflict the helping professionals, whether in an evaluation or treatment role. In addition, the process is faulty because child abuse and family relationships do not lend themselves to the black-and-white definitions under the law and because guilt or blame do not resolve the problem.

However necessary the legal processing of abuse and neglect may be, it makes remediation more difficult.

It would, of course, be helpful if all parents who abuse their children had the courage and insight to confront the problem directly (as some do) and work cooperatively with both the legal and remedial agencies or systems. Since this happens in only a minority of the cases, it is necessary to work with the situation as it is presented.

Foster-parenting. This is one of the essential elements of the system. Given that there will be instances where children will need protection and out-of-home care, either temporarily or on a more long-term basis, foster parents become a very important, though sometimes neglected, element in the abuse or neglect situation. There is a desperate need for more and better-trained foster homes to temporarily protect children while their parents are getting help.

Foster parents are helpful and self-sacrificing to the point, at times, of being heroic. They open their hearts and their homes to damaged, and at times damaging, children. They, however, are often offered little help with their charges, are often required to make financial sacrifices to care for them, and at times they have attitudes that are counterproductive. Foster parents often see themselves as rescuers of children and have little understanding or empathy for the children's parents. Frequently they are poorly prepared to cope with the damage done to the children they receive, and are too often not involved in an overall plan of action to return the children to the parents. They become attached to some children and can become enmeshed in the adversary struggles over the eventual return of the children to the natural parents.

While at one time the "volunteer" nature of foster parenting was appropriate, abused children come with such severe problems and such complex intra-family issues that a new breed of adequately compensated and professionally trained foster parents is needed. This kind of foster parenting has been adopted and promoted in some locations across the land, but it needs to be expanded greatly. Foster parents are needed who can play a therapeutic role in remediating the child's problems, can prepare children for return to the natural parents, and can negotiate the maze of legal, medical, and social systems.

Professionals. These include physicians, nurses, counselors, psychologists, and social workers, as well as other involved professionals, all of whom need more adequate and specific training around issues of child abuse and the dynamics of child-abusing families. Most professional training about child abuse, where it is provided at all, offers survey material and bits and pieces of training around the issue. Most professionals have to get their training and understanding of abusing families and abuse through on-the-job training. While there is no substitute for this kind of training, higher-education programs that train health care professionals need to offer more complete training in this area.

Preventive Efforts. Through public awareness programs, preventive efforts have been extensive. Media presentations via public service announcements and dramatic presentations have increased over the past several years and have undoubtedly resulted in increased public awareness. Those that have had the greatest impact—i.e., dramatic presentations (movies and series)—have unfortunately tended to perpetuate myths. They tend to draw a black-and-white contrast between perpetrator and victim; they tend to focus on sensational acts of abuse and do not paint an accurate picture of the psychological and behavioral consequences to victims, the antecedent experiences of the abuser, or the grinding, damaging reality of the unsensational but equally damaging experiences of continuous psychological and nondramatic physical abuse. The dramatizations are often painted in such vivid colors that it is too easy for the viewer to ascribe the abuse problem to unusual circumstances, "other people," or "other communities." While they are less exotic and perhaps less appealing, the less interesting realities of abuse and the less glamorous and appealing aspects of the consequences to abused children are necessary for the general community to understand.

It is common wisdom that it is better to prevent problems than to fix, remediate, or treat them after they have developed. This is easier said than done when applied to child abuse, since the seeds of abuse are scattered throughout our society in various stages of germination and the roots extend through generations of attitudes, problems, and behavior patterns. Prevention of child abuse has no single answer, yields no easy solution, and involves our society at all levels of endeavor. Prevention of child abuse can be considered at three different levels. They may be labeled *primary, secondary,* and *tertiary* (third-level) prevention.

Primary prevention requires creating or controlling the attitudes, stresses, and personality variables that are causative factors in abuse so that no abuse of children occurs. In some respects, the task of primary prevention is analogous to preventing bad weather. We have some knowledge of the forces and processes that lead to abuse, but was cannot measure and predict them with the precision necessary for prevention. Even if or when we could accomplish such precision, it is not likely that we would be willing to apply the social and political power that would be required to control or channel these variables. We cannot require people to marry only people with whom they are compatible. We cannot require people to delay having children until they demonstrate adequate parenting skills. We cannot require people to obtain treatment for emotional or mental problems except within very narrow limits and for limited ends.

What is left to us is educating the community about effective parenting, stress management, available resources for help with personal problems, and other pertinent information. While local efforts at such community education have some impact, to be truly effective this educational effort would have to become a campaign of the magnitude of those used in selling Sugar Pops or Toyota cars.

Secondary prevention consists of preventing further abuse where there has been some occasional abuse or where there are the beginnings of an abusive pattern. In most instances, this occurs in families in which there are unusual stresses, where the parent's personality problems are not profound, and where the abuse causes distress to the abusing parent and is seen by him or her as a problem. A prevention program at this level should include the community education referred to under primary prevention, but, in addition, the required availability and accessibility of helping resources and in some cases protecting intervention through legal entities such as CPS and the courts. This intervention is necessary for temporary protection of the child and to provide some impetus for the parent to seek required remedial help.

Helping resources should be viewed in a broad context and include such things as personal support through self-help programs, such as Parents Anonymous, parent education, personal counseling, financial planning, job placement and training, and respite care for children during periods of peak stress. While most of these elements are available to some degree in our communities, they tend to be fragmented, not highly coordinated, and probably not as extensive, accessible, or flexible as would be ideal. In the area of counseling services, there are indications that the helping professionals have not developed a variety of skills needed to deal effectively with child abuse. Professional education programs, as stated earlier, provide little in the area of training about child abuse. The weekly office-visit format that is dictated by tradition and economics is usually not the most effective.

Tertiary prevention refers to the prevention of continued abuse by families whose abuse has been extensive and prolonged and where the abusive parents, either because of training, defensiveness, or personal pathology, do not see the abuse as wrong or damaging to the child. Prevention at this level subsumes the programs outlined under primary and secondary prevention, with a stronger emphasis on legal intervention and more frequent separation of the child from the parents. It also requires more intensive psychological or psychiatric services. Tertiary prevention frequently places us, and, more important, the child in a no-win situation. While a child's attitudes, capabilities, and future life are distorted and warped by a pattern of abuse, separation from the parents (however abusive) is often a frightening and damaging event. There is no solution to this dilemma other than to weigh carefully the potential effects of the risk of continued abuse versus the damage caused by separation by the parents and then select the lesser of two evils.

It is obvious that adequate programming for the problem of child abuse in our society requires a more organized and concerted effort than has been the case so far, and in spite of the cost it will require more resources. Child abuse is a catastrophic cross-generational disease. Our choices are to pay the price for prevention, intervention, and treatment—or live with it.

The problem of child abuse is with us for the foreseeable future. While nothing presents itself as a final solution, there are things that can be done for families that are caught in its deadly grip. These things require empathy and patience but also creative, active intervention. At times, the psychological pathology that results from and contributes to abuse can be treated. Parents can learn and be taught constructive ways to cope with both child behavior problems and life stresses. At times, the child can and must be made safe by removal from the home, but this should be the last resort and every effort should be made to reunify the child with his family in a manner that is consistent with safety for the child. Those of us who are professionals should continue to seek solutions and effective remediation for the abuse cycle.

Suggested Reading

Dreikurs, R. and Gray, L. 1968. *A New Approach To Discipline: Logical Consequences.* New York: Hawthorne Books, Inc.

Elmer, E. 1977. *Children In Jeopardy,* fourth edition. Pittsburgh: University of Pittsburgh Press.

Gil, D. G. 1978. *Violence Against Children.* Cambridge, MA: Harvard University Press.

Giovannoni, J. and Becerra, R. 1979. *Defining Child Abuse.* New York: Free Press.

Helfer, R. E. and Kempe, R. S. 1987. *The Battered Child,* fourth edition. Chicago: University of Chicago Press.

Justice, B. and Justice, R. 1976. *The Abusing Family.* New York: Human Services Press.

Kadoshin, A. and Martin, J. A. 1981. *Child Abuse: An Interactional Event.* New York: Columbia University Press.

Kempe, C. H. and Helfer, R. E. 1974. *Helping the Battered Child and His Family.* Philadelphia: Lippincott.

Kempe, R. S. and Kempe, C. H. 1978. *Child Abuse.* Cambridge, MA: Harvard University Press.

Pragelow, M. D. 1984. *Family Violence.* New York: Praeger.

THE CROSSROAD COUNSELING LIBRARY
Books of Related Interest

James Archer, Jr.
COUNSELING COLLEGE STUDENTS
A Practical Guide for Teachers, Parents, and Counselors
"Must reading for everyone on campus—professors,
administrators, dorm personnel, chaplains, and friends—as
well as parents and other counselors to whom college students
turn for support."—*Dr. William Van Ornum* $17.95

Denyse Beaudet
ENCOUNTERING THE MONSTER
Pathways in Children's Dreams
Based on original empirical research, and with recourse to the
works of Jung, Neumann, Eliade, Marie-Louise Franz, and
others, this book offers proven methods of approaching and
understanding the dream life of children. $19.95

Robert W. Buckingham
CARE OF THE DYING CHILD
A Practical Guide for Those Who Help Others
"Buckingham's book delivers a powerful, poignant message
deserving a wide readership."—*Library Journal* $17.95

Sidney Callahan
PARENTS FOREVER
You and Your Adult Children
An award-winning writer, psychologist, and mother of six
adult children offers reassurance and wisdom to millions of
other parents who never knew it would go on for so long....
$19.95

John Gerdtz and Joel Bregman, M. D.
AUTISM
A Practical Guide for Those Who Help Others
An up-to-date and comprehensive guidebook for everyone
who works with autistic children, adolescents, adults, and their
families. Includes latest information on medications. $17.95

Virginia Curran Hoffman
THE CODEPENDENT CHURCH
From Dysfunctional Religious Family to Genuine Faith Community
How to recognize and overcome one's codependence on a
religious group through a twelve-step process of spiritual
understanding. $11.95 paperback

Marion Howard
HOW TO HELP YOUR TEENAGER
POSTPONE SEXUAL INVOLVEMENT
Based on a national educational program that works, this book
advises parents, teachers, and counselors on how they can help
their teens resist social and peer pressures regarding sex.
$9.95 paperback

Marion Howard
SOMETIMES I WONDER ABOUT ME
Teenagers and Mental Health
Combines fictional narratives with sound, understandable
professional advice to help teenagers recognize the difference
between serious problems and normal problems of adjustment.
$9.95 paperback

Charles H. Huber and Patricia G. Driskill
FAMILY THERAPY
A Basic Guide for the Helping Professions
A lively primer for all professional helpers on treating the
family as a system. $18.95

Eugene Kennedy
SEXUAL COUNSELING
A Practical Guide for Those Who Help Others
Newly revised and up-to-date edition of an essential book on
counseling people with sexual problems, with a new chapter
on the counselor and AIDS. $17.95

Judith M. Knowlton
HIGHER POWERED
A Ninety Day Guide to Serenity and Self-Esteem
"A treasure! Not only those in recovery, but everyone seeking
peace and self-assurance will benefit from the ideas and
inspiration in this excellent book."—*Thomas W. Perrin*
$9.95 paperback

Bonnie Lester
WOMEN AND AIDS
A Practical Guide for Those Who Help Others
Provides positive ways for women to deal with their fears, and
to help others who react with fear to people who have AIDS.
$15.95

Robert J. Lovinger
RELIGION AND COUNSELING
The Psychological Impact of Religious Belief
How counselors and clergy can best understand the important
emotional significance of religious thoughts and feelings.
$17.95

Sophie L. Lovinger, Mary Ellen Brandell, and
Linda Seestedt-Stanford
LANGUAGE LEARNING DISABILITIES
*A New and Practical Approach for Those Who Work with Children
and Their Families*
Here is new information, together with practical suggestions,
on how teachers, therapists, and families can work together to
give learning disabled children new strengths. $22.95

Helen B. McDonald and Audrey I. Steinhorn
UNDERSTANDING HOMOSEXUALITY
A Guide for Those Who Know, Love, or Counsel Gay and Lesbian Individuals
A sensitive guide to better understanding and counseling gay men, lesbians, and their parents, at every stage of their lives.
$10.95 paperback

James McGuirk and Mary Elizabeth McGuirk
FOR WANT OF A CHILD
A Psychologist and His Wife Explore the Emotional Effects and Challenges of Infertility
A new understanding of infertility that comes from one couple's lived experience, as well as sound professional advice for couples and counselors. $14.95

Janice N. McLean and Sheila A. Knights
PHOBICS AND OTHER PANIC VICTIMS
A Practical Guide for Those Who Help Them
"A must for the phobic, spouse and family, and for the physician and support people who help them."—*Arthur B. Hardy, M. D., Founder, TERRAP Phobia Program* $17.95

John B. Mordock and William Van Ornum
CRISIS COUNSELING WITH CHILDREN AND ADOLESCENTS
A Guide for Nonprofessional Counselors
New Expanded Edition
"Every parent should keep this book on the shelf right next to the nutrition, medical, and Dr. Spock books."—*Marriage & Family Living* $12.95

John B. Mordock
COUNSELING CHILDREN
Basic Principles for Helping the Troubled and Defiant Child
Helps counselors consider the best route for a particular child, and offers proven principles and methods to counsel troubled children in a variety of situations. $17.95

Cherry Boone O'Neill
DEAR CHERRY
Questions and Answers on Eating Disorders
Practical and inspiring advice on eating disorders from the
best- selling author of *Starving for Attention.*
$8.95 paperback

Thomas W. Perrin
I AM AN ADULT WHO GREW UP IN AN ALCOHOLIC
FAMILY
At once moving and practical, this long-awaited book by a
leader in the addiction field provides new hope to other adult
children of alcoholics and those who love them.
$8.95 paperback

Dianne Doyle Pita
ADDICTIONS COUNSELING
A Practical Guide to Counseling People
with Chemical and Other Addictions
"A fresh and greatly needed approach to helping the whole
person—it fills a great gap in the existing literature."—*Thomas*
Perrin $17.95

Paul G. Quinnett
ON BECOMING A HEALTH
AND HUMAN SERVICES MANAGER
A Practical Guide for Clinicians and Counselors
A new and essential guide to management for everyone in the
helping professions—from mental health to nursing, from
social work to teaching. $19.95

Paul G. Quinnett
SUICIDE: THE FOREVER DECISION
For Those Thinking About Suicide,
and For Those Who Know, Love, or Counsel Them
New Expanded Edition
"A treasure— this book can help save lives."—*Dr. William Van*
Ornum $9.95 paperback

Paul G. Quinnett
WHEN SELF-HELP FAILS
A Guide to Counseling Services
"Without a doubt one of the most honest, reassuring, and useful self-help books ever."—*Booklist* $11.95 paperback

Judah L. Ronch
ALZHEIMER'S DISEASE
A Practical Guide for Families and Other Caregivers
Must reading for everyone who must deal with the effects of this tragic disease on a daily basis. $11.95 paperback

Theodore Isaac Rubin, M. D.
ANTI-SEMITISM: A Disease of the Mind
"A most poignant and lucid examination of a severe emotional disease. A splendid job!"—*Dr. Herbert S. Strean* $17.95

Theodore Isaac Rubin, M. D.
CHILD POTENTIAL
Fulfilling Your Child's Intellectual, Emotional, and Creative Promise
A treasury of fresh ideas for parents to help their children become their best selves. $17.95 hardcover $11.95 paperback

E. Fritz Schmerl, M. D. with Sally Patterson Tubach
THE CHALLENGE OF AGE
A Guide to Growing Older in Health and Happiness
"A practical, commonsensical guide for all ages."—*Booklist*
$14.95 paperback

Judy Schwarz
ANOTHER DOOR TO LEARNING
True Stories of Learning Disabled Children and Adults, and the Keys to Their Success
With Illustrations by Carol Stockdale
Fascinating true stories that celebrate the journeys of atypical learners, and what parents and teachers can do to make a lasting difference in their lives. $18.95

John R. Shack
COUPLES COUNSELING
A Practical Guide for Those Who Help Others
An essential guide to dealing with the 20 percent of all
counseling situations that involve a relationship. $15.95

Milton F. Shore, Patrick J. Brice, and Barbara G. Love
WHEN YOUR CHILD NEEDS TESTING
What Parents, Teachers, and Other Helpers Need to Know about
Psychological Testing
A helpful map to the world of psychological testing that will
ease fears and encourage better decision making among
parents and others who care for children and adolescents.
$18.95

Herbert S. Strean as told to Lucy Freeman
BEHIND THE COUCH
Revelations of a Psychoanalyst
"An entertaining account of an analyst's thoughts and
feelings."—*Psychology Today* $11.95 paperback

Stuart Sutherland
THE INTERNATIONAL DICTIONARY OF PSYCHOLOGY
This new dictionary of psychology also covers a wide range of
related disciplines, from anthropology to sociology. $49.50

Joan Leslie Taylor
IN THE LIGHT OF DYING
The Journals of a Hospice Volunteer
"Beautifully recounts the healing (our own) that results from
service to others, and might well be considered as required
reading for hospice volunteers."—Stephen Levine, author of
Who Dies? $17.95

William Van Ornum and Mary W. Van Ornum
TALKING TO CHILDREN ABOUT NUCLEAR WAR
"A wise book. A needed book. An urgent book."
—*Dr. Karl A. Menninger*
$14.95 hardcover $9.95 paperback